RIDING STANDING UP

A MEMOIR

SPARROW SPAULDING

Cage Free Publishing

Houston

Some names and other identifying characteristics of the people included in this memoir have been changed.

Library of Congress number has been applied for.

Riding Standing Up by Sparrow Spaulding, 1st edition
ISBN 978-1-7324512-0-9

For Raven

If you find the mirror of the heart dull, the rust has not been cleared from its face.

—*Rumi*

Acknowledgements

I'd like to deeply thank everyone who has played a role in the drama called "my life." You have played your roles perfectly.

Author's Note

This book is also dedicated to anyone who grew up with parents who smoked in the car with the windows rolled up.

RIDING STANDING UP

A MEMOIR

Chapter 1

Life was perfect. And when I say perfect I mean it in every sense of the word. A fairy tale. I'd even go as far as to say life was like that proverbial bowl of cherries—without the pits, even.

When I was little I lived in a beautiful house with a loving mom, all the toys a girl could want, and a dad who was there when he wasn't working or out with the guys. My maternal grandparents worshiped me. I was a pleasant child, healthy and smart for my age. My biggest problems in life were wondering why people were singing to me on my birthday—it freaked me out—and not liking how Mom put my potty chair in the middle of the living room in front of the TV. I felt a bit exposed.

My mother was the most beautiful being I had ever laid eyes on. She had these amazing dark brown doe eyes and long, black hair. Stick straight. I later found out she ironed it with the same iron she used to iron Dad's shirts though I never saw her do it. She was petite, almost waifish, and seemed to glide instead of walk when coming toward me.

Mom was always smiling and giving me hugs and kisses. Every day she told me how much she loved me and every night she read me my favorite books. *Are You My Mother* was about a bird that leaves the nest in search of its mama. He goes around town asking everyone he meets, "Are you my mother?" They all answer no. Just when the bird is about to give up a big crane comes along, scoops it up, and puts it right back in its nest. Moments later its mother returns with food for her baby bird and all ends well.

Hooray for Henry was about a young boy who is at his school's field day. He puts off eating any of the wonderful food because he is so intent on winning a prize, but he doesn't win anything and when he finally decides to eat all of the food is gone. Disappointed, he is about to leave when he hears there is one last contest—the pie-eating contest. He decides to enter, wins the contest and gets a prize. I loved hearing the happy endings of these books and I always went to sleep with a smile on my face.

Mom never once got mad at me. Even when I sneaked off to poop in my big-girl panties, too intimidated to sit on a potty out in the open, she understood. She called out, "Spar-row, where are you?" as she wandered through the bedrooms. She always found me in the same hiding spot; underneath the Raggedy Ann table and chairs set in my room. I thought I was invisible under there. I could never figure out how she found me.

When Mom went to work at a local beauty salon Grandma would come over to watch my younger brother Mikey and me. I loved being with my grandmother. She used to sing to me, though most times it was in Italian and I didn't understand it. I followed her like a baby duckling. I remember loving her scent—a blend of oregano and sweat, with a touch of something sweet. My aunt said it was her diabetes that gave her that sweet smell but I loved it just the same.

As I told you, life was perfect. I was an enchanted princess, as all two-year-olds are supposed to be.

Chapter 2

Life was still cherries the day it happened. It didn't matter that Dad was no longer living with us and that I didn't know where Mikey was—for the first time in almost a year I had Mom all to myself. She doted on me and never let me out of her sight. I reveled in every minute of the extra love and attention she lavished on me. Being a curious kid I must have asked at some point where the "boys" were and Mom probably gave some vague response like, "You'll see them soon, Sparrow."

I was feeling extra happy that morning because we were on our way to get donuts. Mom and I were holding hands in the parking lot when it happened. Dad ambushed us from behind. In one fell swoop he shoved my mother to the ground hard with his right arm and scooped me up forcefully with his left. I didn't realize it was my own father stealing me until he tossed me into the backseat of the car and I saw his manic face.

My eyes were on Mom as she lay twisted on the pavement, hurt and screaming. "Mommy!" I cried as I beat my palms against the glass, wailing from the depths of my little soul. Dad hurried into the driver's seat and sped away. As Mom got smaller and smaller my terror grew because I feared I wouldn't see her again for a very long time.

I don't remember the entire car ride to Nana's house. Well, trailer. She lived in a tiny town in upstate New York so it took a few hours to get there. I heaved and sobbed for a very long time and must have cried myself to sleep.

Nana was Dad's mom and truth be told I never liked her. She was an uptight woman with silver hair and flaming red lips. And the lady liked her booze. She was the local Avon rep so she always smelled like a toxic combination of cheap perfume and even cheaper gin.

Nana had a stiff face. Botox wasn't on the market yet, but when she smiled she looked like someone was sticking a gun to her head and ordering her to smile. She never smiled with her eyes, at least not in my presence. She must have had her reasons, but try telling that to a three-year-old.

To make matters worse she also played the organ. Badly. Perhaps she was good at it and I just hated the sound. The music was eerie and became downright ear-piercing when her gray poodle Montague howled along.

Nana wasn't playing the organ when we arrived, but she was drinking and has that stiff look on her face. Mikey was sleeping in a playpen in the living room.

"What are you gonna do now?" she asked.

"I'm taking the kids down South."

"You're outta your goddamned mind."

She didn't seem happy with him even though Mom swore Nana couldn't stand her. Mom had grown up in the city and my dad was from the sticks. His family couldn't handle my mom's big hair, overdone makeup, and brightly painted talons she called fingernails. And I'm sure Mom didn't have an outdoorsy bone in her body. Even so I don't think Nana approved of Dad's decision to kidnap his own children.

Chapter 3

Mom won't talk about her past these days. Even if I ask delicately it usually ends up with her crying and saying she has to go. I've asked questions over the years and have gotten some answers but to be honest there are still details that will forever remain fuzzy.

My mom was born in 1950 and grew up in a rundown neighborhood near Harlem that was mostly Italian and Hispanic. She was the third of four children, beautiful and full of life. She was a devout Catholic girl and spent much of her time with the nuns at church. Her dream was to join the convent but her mother told her, in no uncertain terms, she was to get married and have babies like all good Italian girls.

When she was twelve her parents decided to leave the city and move to Long Island. It wasn't the booming place it is today. From what I gather it was much like moving to the country. They purchased a modest three-bedroom house and she lived there until she married my father.

When Mom hit her teenage years she became rebellious. Her parents were overbearing and she wouldn't stand for it. They say middle children either become peacemakers or problem children. Mom definitely became the latter, especially when compared with her two older siblings who never disobeyed. Mom's older sister, Maria, was overweight and hirsute, and according to Mom a total bookworm with zero friends. She never gave her parents any grief. They didn't get along at all, which makes me wonder why Mom chose her as my godmother. I guess she didn't have much choice. Mom's older brother, Antonio was a good Italian mama's boy who never did anything wrong in his parents' eyes either, unless you count forcing himself on Mom and taking her virginity, but she never told a soul about that.

Mom admits she got married in order to get out of the house. She was introduced to Dad by a relative and the sparks flew—at least for Dad. Mom was, in fact, taken with my father, who could be quite charming in his way, but her true love and high school sweetheart had gone to Vietnam and she was left with tough choices. She chose Dad.

Dad was born in upstate New York in 1946. His dad was French Canadian and his mother was English. I know almost nothing of my father's youth except for one story of how his mother tied him to a tree when he was out of control. I don't recall who told me that story, though if true, it would explain a lot. I also heard that my dad never actually graduated high school but instead joined the Navy. Word was he had gotten into some trouble.

He was the third of four children also, just like Mom. He was whip smart but not very disciplined. Dad could build anything, fix anything, and solve the world's problems. He was handsome and a smooth talker—a real charmer. He just couldn't control his drinking or philandering. Or his vengeful, scheming mind.

Dad also grew up Catholic and was an altar boy. It wasn't a great experience for him. He renounced all religion in his adulthood and when he would have one too many drinks he would talk shit about this one priest who used to make Dad wash his feet. I've often wondered what else he had to wash.

On the surface it must have seemed like my parents were the perfect couple. They were both attractive, up-and-coming and easily the best-dressed pair in any room. They had a nice home, two dogs, and a boy and a girl. We were a seventies bell bottom version of a Norman Rockwell painting.

Even though Dad had a temper and liked his drink Mom said they would have stayed together had it not been for the cheating. Mom told me how she found little hints here and there, but of course this was before cell phones and the internet so all she had to go on were clues—a number in his wallet, a matchbook from an out-of-the-way bar. After several years of wondering, she finally decided to set my father up and see if he'd take the bait. She convinced an attractive girlfriend to approach my father at one of his local hangouts and try to take him home. Her brilliant plan worked and my mother was waiting in the parking lot as Dad walked out of the bar with his arm around Mom's friend. He was caught red-handed. She described how he tried to make excuses and talk his way out of it but she was done.

Dad was devastated and did everything he could to get her back. He was one of those men who really loved the idea of a wife and family and thought there was nothing wrong with an occasional piece on the side. He was a successful salesman and believed his duties as husband ended with providing an upper-middle-class lifestyle. He couldn't sell that philosophy to Mom.

It wasn't long after that Mom reconnected with Frank, her high school sweetheart. Mom dated quite a bit in school but Frank was her one true love. He was back from Vietnam. Shot in the chest, in shell-shock, addicted to heroin and alcohol. And still in love with Mom.

Dad moved out and quite soon after Frank moved in. The house was rather empty because Dad took a lot of the furniture. It was drafty and cold, but that could have been because someone left a window open. Or maybe Mom didn't pay the electric bill. Frank's brother Artie stayed over from time to time but I don't know where he slept—most likely on the sofa.

Mom said Dad was overcome with jealousy and rage when he was replaced so quickly, especially with someone from her past. Dad said Mom was partying and not taking care of my brother and me properly. I'm sure both are a little true. I do know Mom was awarded custody of us in the divorce. But the law didn't matter to my dad. He was a rule-breaker from day one. Dad did what (and who) he wanted to do. A few years back I found out from Dad's second wife that he confessed to cheating on my mother on their honeymoon. Mom was in the hotel salon getting her hair styled and Dad had his way with the chamber maid.

I've heard from more than one family member that kidnapping my brother and me was not my dad's idea. It was my grandmother's plan. No, not Nana—she was too busy with her Beefeater and Skin So Soft. I'm referring to Mom's mom, who was so small and cute that everyone called her Bunny. Why would a mother help her son-in-law steal her own daughter's children? It seems so outrageous and cruel, like something that would take place on an episode of *Dynasty* or in a Lifetime movie of the week— not in *real* life.

I don't know why she did it. Or how she convinced my grandfather to go along with her scheme. All I have are bits and pieces. Over the years I have put some key elements together and a few things make sense, sort-of.

For many reasons my grandparents grew to resent my mother. She became the family scapegoat. She was the middle child, sweet and quiet at first, excited to one day join the convent. But it wasn't long before puberty came and she blossomed into a stunning young woman. By the time she was fifteen everyone was taking notice of her, including her brother.

I don't know how old she was when the abuse started but she insisted it went on a long time. I can't imagine that no one else knew about it considering the tiny house her family lived in, but I wasn't there and can only guess at these things. There were three girls and one boy and if you know anything about Italian mothers and their sons they are right up there with the Pope. I asked Mom several times over the years why she didn't tell someone what was going on and she always accused me of "blaming the victim." I wasn't trying to blame her; I just wanted to know what stopped her from standing up for herself. She never gave me an answer.

It's possible her brother was putting the moves on their older sister too. Mom told me a rhyme he taunted Maria with when their parents weren't around:

Maria, Maria, don't say no
Down the cellar we will go
Put your ass against the wall
Here I come balls and all
Won't your mother be surprised
When she sees your belly rise
Won't your father be disgusted
When he sees your cherry's busted.

Lord only knows how many cherries my uncle busted, especially within his own family. It might explain why Maria went on to eventually develop Paranoid Schizophrenia. The story is that she drove her husband so crazy with her delusional ways he killed himself with a shot gun in their minivan at the nearby landfill.

I always loved Uncle Duke. He was kind and even-tempered. I was starting college at the time and Maria had called to tell me she wanted to help pay my tuition with the insurance money. I said "No, thank you" and never spoke to her again. Even at that age there was no way I wanted anything to do with blood money.

By the time Mom was sixteen she had discovered boys, or they discovered her. She dated a lot and used to tell me stories of how her parents would embarrass her when boys came over. One story that sticks out is how my grandmother refused to take down the garlic she hung over the front door to ward off evil spirits. Mom says it reeked and she often dated Jewish boys, like Jimmy Cline, who didn't understand her family's superstitions. Mom said she refused to date Italians because she had grown up with enough "greasy Guineas" around and couldn't stand the "hairy bastards," which infuriated her parents.

Mom went from rebellious to defiant in her teen years and would sneak out, stay out past curfew, and hang out with friends—boys and girls—her parents didn't approve of—which was pretty much everyone. Mom said unless they were fat and Italian her parents wouldn't accept them. She also had a lot of black friends which caused her father to become unglued. They weren't allowed at the house, not that she would ever invite them. Mom was too ashamed of the yelling and fighting that went on in her home so she kept everyone away as much as possible.

Mom smoked cigarettes, wore miniskirts, and mouthed off when she felt attacked. She had big hair, heavy eyeliner, and tall shoes. Her parents thought the best way to handle her was to raise their voices and fists. Mom told me a story of how she had come home late one night and her father was waiting up for her. He hid behind the door and as she was sneaking in he grabbed her, threw her down and kicked the shit out of her. Repeatedly.

Mom graduated high school in 1968 and enrolled in beauty school. She became quite a successful cosmetologist and had her career launched when she met Dad. He charmed my grandparents effortlessly. They saw him as the man who would tame Mom and force her to settle down. Though he wasn't Italian they overlooked it because he was Catholic. And he had that winning smile.

It seemed like things were going fairly well for a while. Mom and Dad settled into their house after the wedding. Mom says she tried real hard to have me. Sadly, she had a miscarriage almost a year before I came along. It was horrible for her because her baby fell into the toilet while she was peeing. Dad was away on a ski trip and Mom freaked out, fished out the baby (I don't know with what) and took herself to the hospital—but not before she packed a bag and put on a full face of makeup. She said she wasn't going to the hospital looking like some wombat. When she got there she put on her best nightgown and smoked cigarettes in her hospital bed. She said the doctor told her it was fine. I often wonder what life would have been like with an older sister. Evidently it was a girl.

Mom was ecstatic when she found out I was also a girl. Her pregnancy was uneventful but she told me over and over how she almost died giving birth to me because she hemorrhaged. Mom was small-framed and still tiny at nine months pregnant. Her labor was excruciating and long and she is still traumatized by it even though she had three more children after me. A few years back when I told her I wanted to have kids someday her advice was to have a C-section. "Don't rough up your muff, Sparrow. Trust me, you'll be sorry." I often don't know what to make of Mom's advice.

Mom was in love with me from the moment she laid eyes on me. I have a stack of memories of her always being there and loving me to pieces. Mom threw me the most lavish birthday parties with lots of decorations and presents. My favorite gift was a baby doll I named Kiki. She was almost as big as me, but I carried her around everywhere. I drew on her face and gave her a crew cut but I just thought it made her more beautiful. I loved her unconditionally, just like Mom loved me.

When Mom decided to leave Dad her parents became outraged. There was no such thing as divorce in our family. All they could ask was how could Mom break up her family for a long-haired hippie veteran? Everyone knows how Vietnam vets were treated when they came home from the war, and it wasn't good. My grandparents certainly weren't grateful that he defended our nation. And his unemployed ass was no match for my father's three-piece suits with that long hair, the motorcycle boots, and the t-shirt he wore of a dog sticking up his middle paw finger with a caption that read *Fetch this.*

Mom shared a story about how she and Frank went to her parents' house to try to talk with them and my grandfather came out waving a rifle. "Get the hell out of here!" he threatened. "I'll kill you both!" At first it seemed unbelievable that my grandfather could have such contempt, but then I remembered how he used to put rubber snakes in his front yard to scare away his two grandsons, my cousins Carlo and Pauly, who lived around the corner. Both were deemed "slow" and my grandfather wanted nothing to do with them. He would complain that they'd come over and eat all the Entenmann's so he scared them off with fake reptiles. I recall them being in their teens and still afraid of those stupid things. Last I heard they never left home though both are in their forties now. They never married or even dated but Pauly has been arrested a few times for visiting happy ending massage parlors. The poor guy can't even get a hand job without drama.

Chapter 4

Dad decided to take my brother and me to Alabama. We were in hiding but Dad knew the warrant for his arrest was only for the state of New York and no one was going to look for us in swampland. We moved in with Dad's older brother Dan who was married with four kids and a vicious attack Chihuahua named Tippy.

Tippy was old, mean, smelly and always growling. He had a huge tumor on his stomach that dragged on the floor when he walked. I think the extra weight was what labored his breathing—that and the incessant barking. It perpetually sounded like he was taking his last breath. Not to mention no one had cut the dog's claws...*ever*. They were so long they turned into curlicues that pointed up in the air and reminded me of the ribbon you curl when you're wrapping a birthday present. The worst part about Tippy was you never knew where he was hiding. You could be headed to the bathroom and turn a corner to find an angry, snarling dog just waiting to eat you alive. That was pretty much a daily occurrence. I lived in constant fear of that dog.

In my new unkempt home I lived with four older cousins. Three of them were sweet but cousin Darla had it in for me. She was five years older than me and was the baby of the family. Darla wasn't happy that she suddenly she had to share her room and toys with me, her three-year-old cousin she barely knew. I'm sure that would be tough for any kid. She had lots of toys and I came with nothing, not even my Kiki doll.

Darla never really hit or abused me; it wasn't her style. She was crafty and tried to get me when no one was looking. Most of it I could handle, like the time she fed me ex-lax or when she would pop the heads off my dolls (her old ones) when I wasn't looking and hide them. More than once I carried around a baby doll all swaddled up so no one would notice her head was missing. Not even me.

The one thing I couldn't handle was sleeping with her. Darla peed the bed. Every. Single. Night. Though she was around eight years old, she had some condition that made her unable to control her bladder. At least that's what everyone said. She also sucked her thumb at night. She did both of these things until she was about fourteen.

The first time it happened I woke up in the middle of the night feeling wet and cold. Darla was still fast asleep and I couldn't wake her—not that she would have gotten up anyway. I trudged down to the living room where my dad slept.

"Dad," I called as I saw my father sleeping soundly on the sofa. "Dad, wake up." I gently touched his shoulder.

"Huh? What is it?"

"Dad, Darla peed the bed. I'm all wet."

"Go back to sleep." Dad closed his eyes.

"But Dad, I'm all wet."

Dad opened his eyes and looked straight at me.

"Go back to bed!" He turned onto his other side to face the wall so he couldn't see me. I stood there, paralyzed. The worst feeling engulfed me. It made me dizzy and hot and my whole body tingled. I didn't recognize it at the time but now I can identify it as the first time I ever felt worthless.

I stood there for a moment longer, then did what I was told. I marched back upstairs and climbed back into bed in my soggy PJs, next to my chubby brick of a cousin. I never asked for help again.

* * *

My half-life away from Mom was surreal. In one sense it felt like an extended vacation to visit family, except it is no vacation being pissed on nightly and terrorized by an attack Chihuahua. Mom's parents came and visited once and it must have been around Easter because I had an Easter dress and bonnet on in the pictures my grandmother later gave me. It was good to see familiar faces, however it felt weird that everyone was there except Mom. When I asked about her they didn't answer or quickly changed the subject.

Dad eventually got a job so Mikey and I started attending Miss Betty's daycare. It was our first experience in a true daycare facility versus being cared for in someone's home. Mom would occasionally have the neighbor watch my brother and me when she was working, but not very often since my grandmother usually took care of us.

Miss Betty's face is forever burned in my brain. She had short, black hair parted to one side with those deep v sideburns and a round, black mole on her left cheek the size of a pencil eraser. She wore a ton of makeup including heavy eyeliner and painted on lips in various tones of red, fuchsia and coral. Now that I think of it she looked like an angry Liza Minelli—either that or Elvis in drag. It's entirely possible that Miss Betty was a transvestite. When parents were around she had a high-pitched sickly sweet southern drawl, but when it was just us kids she sounded more like a hillbilly version of the Hulk, barking orders like, "Sparrow, go wipe so-and-so's butt."

Since I was responsible for my age and looked after Mikey so well Miss Betty thought I should be in charge of the kids just learning to use the potty. Sometimes I would have to take a break from playing to escort some of the kiddos to the potty room and wait for them to make so I could wipe their little asses and get them back out onto the playground. I didn't mind so much but every once in a while I'd get a real stinker of a kid who probably had too much milk in his diet because the smell would be ungodly. The potty room was small and not at all ventilated. Eventually I learned how to just stop breathing in there but it's a wonder I didn't pass out either from the fumes or lack of oxygen.

The one thing I liked about going to Miss Betty's was that once or twice a week we got to go to the local community pool. Besides the fun of swimming with the other kids the whole excursion broke up the day so it didn't seem like I was spending the whole time with this scary excuse for a nanny.

One morning I was getting dressed and because we were going to the pool that day I thought I would be clever and wear my bathing suit underneath my T-shirt and shorts. That way I would be ready to hit the pool and wouldn't have to go through the whole changing process. Also, I didn't like changing in front of everyone so how brilliant to kill two birds with one stone, right? Everything went seamlessly until we had to change back into our clothes and I discovered I had forgotten to pack underwear. My heart fell into my stomach, then my stomach hit the ground. *I'm so busted*, was all I could think to myself. I went into total panic mode.

Every day when we came back from the pool Miss Betty made all the kids get in line for the underwear check. One by one we walked up to her and she peeked down our shorts to make sure we were wearing our skivvies. I never knew what happened to the kids who weren't wearing theirs because she had them go into another room. The room of shame. I wondered if they got whipped because it seemed like lots of kids I knew in those parts got whipped with the belt. I stood in line with the other kids and let her check to see if I had purple hearts or pink flowers on that day. (Keep in mind I'm referring to Miss Betty as a she but I'm still not certain.)

I felt the adrenaline surge as I was getting closer and closer in line. I broke into a full body sweat—the type of sweat where you get damp in places you didn't know you had sweat glands. I should have told Miss Betty that I forgot my underwear that day but I was too scared to form words. *Almost there. Two kids ahead of me. This is gonna be bad. I wonder if I'll die.* Those were the thoughts racing through my head as I stood in the line of terror. Miss Betty looked down my shorts and seemed shocked that Little Miss Perfect wasn't wearing any underwear. She stopped for a moment, then said, "You'll be fine" and shooed me away.

I'm lucky I've never been the type to piss or shit myself when I'm nervous because that day it would have run right down my leg without any Hello Kitty barrier. What? I'll be fine? The biggest wave of relief washed over me. After that was nap time and as I lay on my little mat I was careful to keep my legs closed so no one could see up my shorts. I was too amped to fall asleep but I was happy to be alive so I was okay lying there, perfectly still, for thirty minutes.

Chapter 5

Out of the blue one day Grandpa Johnny showed up at Uncle Dan's house and said he was taking me to Disney World. He had driven all the way from New York in his Smurf blue AMC Pacer. I loved that little two-door hatchback with the white vinyl interior. Grandpa said he would save it for me so I could have it when I got my driver's license. That seemed eons away but I could picture myself driving it with the windows down and my hair blowing in the breeze. By then I was four and the only reason I know this is because I somehow ended up with a picture of myself blowing out four candles on a Snow White and the Seven Dwarves birthday cake. My uncle's living room is in the background and chubby cousin Darla, sporting a pink party hat, is right next to me eyeing the cake. I received a white plastic tea set that came in a cardboard box with a see-through cellophane front. My hair was long and straight in the picture and I was wearing a grey plaid dress with pleats and pockets in the front. Everything in the picture looked normal.

Grandpa and I drove down the road playing various highway games that involved counting cars and checking license plates. He told me where Mississippi was and how to spell it. He loved spending time with me. He was always patient, kind and very loving toward me. I know he was never like that with his own children so I'm not sure what changed in him. Perhaps it was age that softened him. Or maybe it was because I was the first granddaughter. Whatever the case I ate it up at the time and enjoyed every minute with Grandpa Johnny.

We weren't very far down the road when Grandpa turned to look at me and said,

"I have a surprise for you."

"What is it, Grandpa?" I replied feeling the excitement build in my chest.

"We can go to Disney World or we can go see your mother. It's up to you."

"What? Mom's alive?!" I was shocked. I really thought she was dead, even though I didn't fully know what that meant. Dad said that she was gone and never coming back so perhaps I concluded she was in heaven with Jesus and the angels. For a long time after I was taken I looked at every woman's face I came across thinking *Are you my mother* much like that baby bird from the book. Eventually I gave up because no one even came close to looking like Mom.

"Of course she's alive," he said. "Would you like to go and see her?"

"Yes!" was all I could utter at first. I forgot about Disney World immediately even though I was excited to see Cinderella's castle and meet Mickey and Minnie. My heart was beating out of my chest. *My mother.* My mother was alive and I was going to get to see her, hug her, and smell her hair. I would once again curl up in her lap and she would read me my favorite books. I was over the moon.

My face hurt from smiling so much the whole trip from Alabama to New Jersey. We played games as we drove and stopped at a Howard Johnson's halfway in between. Grandpa got me several Happy Meals from McDonald's along the way, though I couldn't tell you what the toys were.

Grandpa told me we were meeting Mom at Uncle Sal's house. Sal was my grandfather's older brother and the patriarch of our family. He and his wife Gina lived in New Jersey and had a great life with their adopted son, also named Sal. They had a reputation for being the kindest, most well-adjusted people in our family. Sal was my mother's godfather and they had a special bond. I later found out she had gone to him and told him what had happened and that she thought her parents were involved in our kidnapping. Mom said Sal told his brother if he did not return us that he was excommunicated from the family permanently. So Grandpa decided, against Grandma's wishes, to return Mikey and me to Mom.

Returning us was complicated because it was too much for Grandpa to take my two-year-old brother to Disney World. He ended up double-crossing Dad because he had no intentions of taking me there in the first place. After he returned me he gave Mom the address where we were living and she got the police involved. Dad returned my brother peacefully in order to avoid being extradited back to New York and facing jail time for violating the custody order. The jig was up.

My legs were wobbly as I walked up the steps to Uncle Sal's brownstone. I had been on an adrenaline rush for two days and it was starting to take a toll on me. Aunt Gina opened the door and greeted us warmly. We said our hellos and she motioned to the dining room where Mom was sitting in a chair. As soon as she saw me she cried and became a little bit hysterical. It reminded me of the time when I was two and had to get stitches in between my eyes because Mom had slammed on her breaks to avoid a car accident. I was in the back seat sitting on the arm rest and went flying to the front and hit the dash board with my face. Mom was frantic when she noticed blood squirting out of my face every time my heart beat so she pulled over to a gas station and they called an ambulance. Our eight-year-old neighbor Kimmy was with us and she rode in the ambulance with me. When we arrived at the hospital I was rushed into a room. I had nicked an important artery in my face and they needed to close it stat. Since there was no time for luxuries like Novocain I was crying and screaming and Mom was so overwhelmed they had to ask her to leave. Just when I needed her most. Luckily I had a great nurse who held my hand and talked to me the whole time I was being sewn up. But I still wanted my mommy.

Mom unraveled again the day she got me back. She had big tears streaming down her face and her mascara ended up running down her cheeks; it looked like she was crying black rivers. She still hadn't gotten up which I thought was odd because I wanted her to scoop me up like the old days but she didn't and so I just stood there looking at her. My head was happy but my heart was numb. Was this my mother? How could it be? I thought she was gone. All of a sudden I got the idea that maybe she wasn't my real mom after all. She could be an imposter.

I don't know how I knew about imposters at that age. The only thing that comes to mind is maybe I saw something in a cartoon or kids' movie. But I knew people could pretend to be other people so I did what I thought was the smart thing to do— I tried to pull her mask off. Mom asked what I was doing and I told her. "I want to see if you're wearing a mask. How do I know it's really you?" If I thought she had unraveled before I was wrong. At this point she totally lost it. She cried so hard I couldn't understand her response. I was frozen. I so badly wanted to believe it was her but it was too risky. By this time I had walled off my heart well. It had been more than a year since the day I was taken and I had already redefined myself as motherless, just like the baby bird in the book. Now I was getting my happy ending just like that little bird but something wasn't clicking. Don't get me wrong, I was excited to see her. But I had stopped having emotional meltdowns a long time ago. I had stopped feeling. To be more accurate, my heart closed the day I was stolen.

When Mom calmed down she said she wanted to show me something. She had a bag and inside were some of my old toys.

There was a wooden dog with wheels, a play telephone and a book. She brought my old copy of *Are You My Mother*. We tried to get me on her lap but it wasn't as easy as it once was. She was larger. "I'm having a baby," she explained. My mom, who could still be an imposter, was pregnant. I felt betrayed. I couldn't articulate it but I felt slighted. Your kids are ripped away from you and instead of coming to find us you just decide to have more?

I knew all too well what it meant when Mom's belly got big, then out popped a screaming baby that got all her attention. I'm told I was jealous of my brother when he was born and Mom couldn't leave us alone in a room together. One time she did and came back to find me bashing in his little skull with a baseball I had grabbed from my toy bin. In time I grew to love him and when we were taken I became his stand-in mommy but this was different. I wanted Mom to myself for five minutes, even if she was some crazy imposter.

Mom read some of my book to me, but she was too emotional to finish it. I needed her to be strong that day but she wasn't capable. Where was my beautiful, perfect mother, the one I had idealized in my head for well over a year? I had never forgotten what she looked like or smelled like. But I needed her to be strong so I could feel my feelings. I was full of sadness, longing, and disappointment but it wasn't safe to let those emotions out. That day I realized only Mom could have the feelings. I decided to stuff mine down and be strong for her.

Chapter 6

I don't recall much about the day my sister Franky was born except for how round her head was when she was brought home. It was a perfect sphere, kind of like those candlepin bowling balls we bowled with in those days. Mom tried out several nicknames but Pumpkin stuck, which later was reduced to Punky. Mom told me she wanted to name her Christy Ann and would even write it on the back of her pictures but Frank insisted she be his namesake. I guess Mom finally gave in.

Mom called me Sparrow most of the time but she had also given me a nickname—Puppy. She said it was because I had a puppy-dog nose. At first I kind of liked it because when Mom used my nickname it felt like she loved me. She never yelled it like she did my real name. When she called me Puppy her voice was soft and sweet and felt like a hug.

"Are you my puppy girl?" she asked.

"Yes," I always replied, smiling, and panting like a dog with my tongue hanging out and my hands up to resemble paws.

One day Mom was having coffee and cigarettes with Aunt Patty, who was married to Frank's brother Artie and I overheard part of their conversation. I don't know who they were talking about but Mom said, "That woman is so ugly. A real *dog.*" My heart sank and I could feel my face getting hot as I ran to the mirror. Oh no! Tears welled up in my eyes. *Mom calls me Puppy because I'm ugly too!* Puppies are just younger dogs, after all. I was devastated. At five I already knew how to do lots of things. I could sing and dance, I could tie my shoes, and I could do my own hair. I could even take care of my little brother and sister. But I didn't know what to do about ugly. The next time Mom called me Puppy I explained that I knew where the nickname had come from and that I was a five year old with a dog face. She tilted her head back and laughed for what felt like an hour. *Why is my being ugly so funny?* I wondered. Once she collected herself she explained to me that I wasn't ugly at all, I was cute like a little puppy dog. I wasn't buying it. I had already discovered the truth. I was ugly. A dog—just like that woman I heard them talking about. My life was over before it had begun. Andy Gibb, my first real crush, would never want a dog-faced girl. How could I go on? I always thought he and I would get married and dance the Hustle together. Mom had taught it to me and I even had a cute red sweater that said *Do the Hustle* across the front. Not to mention, I couldn't remember one time that someone had said I was pretty. People were always telling Mom how gorgeous she was, but no one ever told me. Not that I could recall, anyway.

I repeatedly asked Mom to stop calling me Puppy but she did not honor my request. She was oblivious to the fact that I cringed every time she said it, so I learned to live with it.

We were living with Frank's parents, Arthur and Lorraine, in New Hampshire when Punky was born. Arthur had a remarkable resemblance (in looks and character) to Archie Bunker with slightly more hair on top and Lorraine was his platinum-blond Edith. Both had that thick, New York accent and Lorraine even screeched a little when she talked. She waited on Arthur like a good Edith, and like a good Archie he never seemed all that appreciative.

They lived in an eighteenth-century farmhouse that had peeling white paint and forest-green trim. It was drafty and the floors creaked when you walked on them. The floor in the kitchen sloped quite a bit so everything looked and felt a little crooked. The house was in a tiny town in the mountains so there wasn't much around. The one place we frequented was called Slick's.

Slick's was a biker bar not far from the house. I don't remember Frank ever having a bike but he dressed the part and all of his friends were bikers. I'm sure Mom didn't want him anywhere near a motorcycle with his drinking. Mom mainly wore the pants in our home which isn't saying much because she freaked out any time she had to make a decision. Mom had two modes: freaked out or checked out. I'm still not sure which one I liked better. At least when she was freaked out she was semi-present. She might yell or cry or point her index finger in your face. She might chase you with a wooden spoon. When she checked out there was no one home. She stared off into space and smoked or curled up in the fetal position on our 1960's-style red floral loveseat with the plastic on (custom plastic, I believe) and faced the wall. Sometimes she slept, and sometimes she masturbated, until one time I called her out. She was lying on her stomach and rubbing her vagina area with both hands over her pants. Then she began moving her butt up and down like she was humping her hands. This made her breathe heavily.

"I know what you're doing, Mom." I was irritated. I knew she was being inappropriate and I was mad that she wasn't being a good role model.

"I'm not doing anything," Mom said. I don't recall her doing it again after that.

We went to Slick's nearly every Sunday. It was our church, I suppose. There were pitchers and pitchers of beer and everyone would tell wild stories and laugh. I used to beg for money for the juke box and played anything by my beloved Andy or the Steve

Miller Band. My first real performance was on a table at Slick's when I was five. I sang and danced to "Jet Airliner" which is a huge deal for a shy kid. I'm sure I had some liquid courage now that I think back since my parents never seemed to mind me having sips of beer.

I never did get close to Arthur and Lorraine. I was intimidated by Lorraine's bright red lips and drawn on eyebrows that had a high, round arch that would have reminded me of Marcel Marceau if I had known who he was at the time. Clearly Lorraine was a fan. She was into ceramics and let me paint ornaments and figurines from time to time. I still have one ornament of a mouse in a stocking with my name at the top. I hang it on the tree every year. It irks me that it never made it into the kiln.

Punky was the best little sister in the world. She never cried, whined or threw fits. Even as a baby she was a dream, always smiling. She didn't talk much but she always knew what was going on. She was typically up for anything and she could always keep up with Mikey and me, first crawling and then running behind us. Everybody loved her.

When it was time for me to enter kindergarten we moved to the next town so we could be closer to the school. It would have taken almost an hour to get to school on a good day from Arthur and Lorraine's house. We moved to a small duplex right in town. We were in the upstairs unit and there was a little girl my age and her mom in the downstairs unit. The girl's name was Hope and she was okay but I didn't really enjoy playing with her. I wasn't used to playing with girls my age and much preferred my new best friend named Morris who lived across the street.

* * *

Every little girl wants to be beautiful for the first day of school and I was no exception. In actuality, I didn't think I could be all that beautiful. I just wanted to look like a human and not a dog-face when meeting my new teacher and classmates. Mom was pissed that I was supposed to start kindergarten because I could already read so she had the school test me and they agreed to let me skip kindergarten altogether. No one knows how I learned to read, not even me. Mom was rather shocked when we went to see Star Wars and I read the beginning out loud. "A long time ago in a galaxy far, far away..." "What? You can read?" she said, more than a little surprised.

I was five when I started first grade and was not emotionally ready to be with the older kids. Not because I threw tantrums or ate paste, but because I was so painfully shy. Mom didn't see that, or if she did it didn't matter. I think she was excited to have me out of the house all day.

The morning of the first day of school I went into the bathroom to see if I could use some of Mom's potions to make myself presentable. Since Mom was beautiful I figured if I did what she did I could be a little like her. I always saw her putting this goopy stuff that came in a metal tube in her long, black hair. Luckily she had left it on the sink next to the toothbrushes. I quickly squeezed the whole tube into my hands and started rubbing it in all over. It didn't take long before I had saturated my whole head. As soon as I looked in the mirror I knew something was wrong. I didn't look a thing like Mom. Instead, I looked like I had just washed my hair with olive oil.

I was nervous but confident that Mom could fix this since Mom did hair for a living. Our apartment was small so I found her in a matter of seconds smoking and having her morning coffee in the living room. I recall having the brief thought that I wish she would stop smoking. It was stinky for one thing, and a few nights back she had accidentally set the couch on fire because she was smoking and removing her nail polish at the same time. I hadn't heard Mom scream that loud since I had been kidnapped. It wasn't a good evening.

"Mom, can you help me?"

"Oh, Sparrow! What did you do?" Mom said, oozing with disappointment.

"I wanted to be pretty like you for school."

"Come on, let's wash your hair." She grabbed my arm and led me back into the bathroom. Mom had me stick my head under the sink as she shocked me with cold water before it warmed. Being a hair stylist she was typically an ace at washing hair. This time she wasn't successful, though I'm not sure how hard she tried.

"God, Sparrow! I can't get this shit out. You're just gonna have to go to school like this. I'll say something to your teacher. Come on, we need to leave soon." Mom sighed and left the room. She needed to finish her cigarette before we went.

When Mom and I walked into my new classroom she bee-lined it to the teacher, dragging me along like a rag doll. I think it would have been better if we had pretended nothing was wrong, because as she was speaking a few kids overheard. Mom clearly wasn't an on-the-spot problem-solver; looking back she should have put my hair in a ponytail and called it good. But she didn't and instead told my teacher how I had used her entire tube of Alberto VO5 in order to make myself beautiful like her.

My teacher had a pained look on her face as she checked out my greasy "do." I felt the embarrassment blossom on my face and work its way down to my toes. To be fair no one made fun of me, though there were a few whispers and some finger-pointing.

I made it through that day and afterward decided I would never like school. *Ever.* That was one decision I remained stubborn about for a very long time.

The only good thing about going to school was that I could stop by Morris's house on the way home. He lived in a light blue ranch-style home directly across the street from me. When we met I liked him instantly and wanted to spend all my free time with him.

Morris Goldmann was an older Jewish man who my mom later told me survived the Holocaust. He lived with his younger sister Deborah who didn't look younger but he was ninety-something and she was eighty-something so it made it tough to tell. I'm not sure if either of them was ever married or had children as I was too young to ask about those things.

There was a lot to like about Morris. He had the whitest hair I had ever seen and he was hunched over so he could be right up in my face when we talked. We would go on walks and find random things to look at under the red magnifying glass he gave me—bugs, leaves, and once some broken glass. His house was filled with trinkets, artifacts and tchotchkes. Morris gave me an English penny that barely fit in the palm of my hand it was so big. I used to hold it and dream of all the things I could buy in England with it. I figured since it was so big it must be worth a lot.

When my birthday rolled around that fall Mom asked who I wanted to invite over.

"I want to have Morris over for dinner."

"Don't you want to invite any kids from class?" I didn't have any friends at school being the shy new kid so the answer was no. I just wanted play time with Morris.

Mom made baked ziti and Morris came over that night with wine for my mom, and flowers and a gift for me. It was the first time anyone had ever bought me flowers and I was elated. For my gift Morris had made a giant tic tac toe set out of wood. I was excited and wanted to play immediately. "Okay, okay let's play," he said with a smile. Turning six felt like a big deal. Not only was it my birthday, but it was also my first official date. I had never felt so special, well not in a long time, at least. It was intoxicating.

That spring Mom told me we were moving into a new house. I was excited at first. My own yard with a swing set and everything. It sounded like a dream until she told me it was far away and I'd be changing schools. Of course my first thought was Morris. We'd grown close and I saw him nearly every day except on the days Deborah answered the door and told me he was napping and couldn't play, but that wasn't very often. Before I could control it tears were streaming down my face. I knew a lot about loss and missing someone so I knew exactly what I was in for. "Don't worry, Sparrow, we'll come back and visit." I knew we wouldn't. Of course I was right.

Our new HUD home was magnificent. Everything in it was brand spanking new (except the furniture) and I got my own room. I picked the smaller room but it had a Smurf-blue carpet that reminded me of Grandpa's Pacer so it was the winner. We had a yard and plenty of room to play. Mom said we were able to get the house because Daddy Frank was a veteran. We lived quite a ways from town and were nestled in the trees. Our street had six houses, actually four houses and two trailers. I was glad we were in a house and not a trailer. Mom said to be grateful our house wasn't on cinderblocks like the neighbors' and I was.

Chapter 7

Summers were a mixed bag for me because on one hand I had to go visit Dad for nearly the entire summer, but on the other hand I usually got to spend a week or two with my mom's parents first. My grandparents were my two favorite people on Earth. Of course at that time I had no idea they were partially responsible for my abduction. I'm glad no one told me.

Even though Johnny and Frances spoke perfect English they were still old school Italian. They yelled, cursed, and threw things at each other, yet they doted on me. I was the first granddaughter and could do no wrong in their eyes. I divided my time between them equally, spending endless hours in the kitchen with my grandmother making various forms of pasta and countless other hours in the front yard with my grandfather. He sat on his bench and listened to AM radio while I climbed trees, discovered bugs and organized my baseball cards.

Grandpa got me into baseball at a young age. He taught me how to throw a curve ball and a knuckle ball and told me all about the Mets. He also taught me about the music he loved. Liza Minelli, the Rat Pack, and his favorite: Bossa Nova. I can't tell you how many times we sang "Girl from Ipanema" together.

On one of those languid summer days I was fairly high up in the maple tree in the front yard while Grandpa was sitting on his bench humming away and reading the paper. A little girl on a cute pink bicycle stopped in front of the house. She had those fancy braids I always liked with different colored hair ties holding them in place and a wide, innocent smile.

"Do you wanna play?" she asked politely.

"Sure," I replied as I quickly made my way down the tree. I was excited to see someone my age because typically there were no kids in my grandparents' neighborhood. Before I made it to the bottom my grandfather bellowed, "Get outta here, Aunt Jemima! You're not welcome here!" He waved his newspaper wildly as if he was swatting at a swarm of hornets. The little girl burst into tears and turned around to ride away before I could even get a word out. I was stunned.

"Grandpa, why can't I play with her? She was being nice!"

"You don't play with negroes," he muttered as he put his newspaper back in order.

I felt the most overwhelming sadness wash over me so I darted into the house to look for my grandmother.

"Grandma, you're not gonna believe what Grandpa just did!" I told her, tears streaming down my face. As I recounted what happened I fully expected her to go outside and give him the what-for like she always did when he did or said something ridiculous. To my surprise, she didn't.

"Your grandfather's right. You don't need to play with *them*." With that she went right back to stirring and humming softly.

Even at seven years old I knew there was something really wrong with that moment. My heart felt like it weighed a thousand pounds and my whole body hurt. I ran into my bedroom and dove head-first into my pillow sobbing for a long time. Mom had always taught us that people come in all sizes, shapes and colors and to never judge anyone by those things. "It's what's inside that counts," I remembered her saying as she pointed to her heart. Why didn't my grandparents see it that way? I wasn't exactly sure, I just knew that how they handled the whole thing was deplorable. I hadn't even noticed what color she was.

We never spoke of that incident but I think that's when I began to pull away a little from my grandparents and realize they were far from perfect. I couldn't name it at that age but I had lost some respect. I still loved them, I just no longer wanted to be like them, which was a problem because I didn't want to be like my parents either.

* * *

Sometimes things happen that seem so outrageous you ask yourself, *Did that really happen?* You could have misinterpreted the situation, although deep down you know you interpreted it correctly but to admit that to yourself might induce a seizure and what good would that do?

One sweltering summer day in Alabama Dad told Mikey and me to get in the car, because we were going for a ride. Mikey and I both climbed into Dad's two-door Ford Bronco. It was tan with navy accents and Dad kept it super clean on the inside and out. That truck sparkled. I kept asking where we were going because any time I was in the car with Dad I was a little apprehensive. Either I remembered the kidnapping or I was worried about his drinking. Dad had no qualms about driving after a lot of drinks and probably had an open beer between his legs about eighty percent of the time. Coors Light, mainly. I'm certain he was drinking on that day. Drinking and smoking with the windows rolled up and the air conditioner blasting, which may explain my still frequent asthma attacks.

"Dad, where are we going?" I asked. Dad was silent. I was riding shotgun and Mikey was in the backseat pouting because I got to sit up front. We kept driving further and further away from civilization and after an hour or so we turned onto a dirt road and eventually came upon some heavily wooded swampland.

"Dad, what are we doing here?" I asked. This time he answered.

"Dad lost a piece off his truck and we need to find it." He often referred to himself in the third person when talking to Mikey and me. Dad parked the truck and told us to get out and start looking for a shiny piece of metal. He pointed in front of us and said, "Start looking over there." I felt uneasy and as I turned around to look at him I saw him reaching under the seat. He pulled out a handgun and my heart pounded.

"Dad, what are you doing with that gun?" I said, my voice shaking. That was the first time I had ever laid eyes on a gun and I was terrified. I felt the complete opposite of safe.

"In case there are snakes," he responded casually. Then Mikey chimed in.

"God, Sparrow, leave Dad alone. Quit being such a baby!" I knew he was teasing but I couldn't focus on his words. I was already processing the situation in my head at lightning speed, trying to figure out if we were in fact in danger and how to protect my mouthy little turd of a brother. I stood there for a moment and pretended to be looking for the car part. It had already dawned on me that where Dad had ordered us to go was way too wooded for any car to drive through. There was no way he could have lost a car part there. That major detail went right over Mikey's head. I watched Dad out of the corner of my eye and saw him looking out onto the water. He looked sad, in a daze. I hadn't seen that look before and it scared me. He looked deranged.

A water moccasin glided across the water. Dad raised his gun to shoot it but I begged him not to. He put the gun back to his side and still looked gone. Just then I heard a voice. It was loud but it came from inside me somehow. It said, "You are in danger! Go to the car!" I didn't waste a second at that point. I figured if I went back to the car I would distract Dad and perhaps get him out of his trance. He probably wouldn't shoot us in his beautiful, super-clean Ford Bronco, anyway.

"Run!" I screamed to Mikey who was laughing at me because he thought I was nuts to be scared of Dad. He didn't remember his own abduction, when Dad picked him up from the neighbor's house before Mom had arrived. From what I was told there was no violence involved and Mikey was only a year old.

I couldn't save Mikey but I was determined to save myself. Dad screwed my life up royally once and I wasn't going to let him finish me off.

I had never run so fast in all my life. As soon as I got to the car I opened the driver's side door and hurled myself in. I locked both doors and tried to catch my breath. My darting to the truck definitely got Dad out of his trance. He and Mikey walked over and Dad beat on the driver side window.

"Get out of there, right now!" he yelled.

"No way!" I felt the slightest bit of reprieve inside the truck and I was staying put. For whatever reason Dad had left the keys inside. Thank God.

After ten to fifteen minutes of Dad vacillating between yelling and cajoling I realized I would have to unlock the car. The sun was setting and we couldn't stay out there in swampland forever. There were no houses or anything nearby and we were on a dirt road. I got the sense I wasn't in imminent danger because Dad no longer had that dazed look, so I unlocked the driver side door after making dad promise we would go straight home and that he would put the gun back under the seat of the car.

Much to my surprise, he did just that. Mikey teased me about it for several minutes but I was really good at tuning him out. It was a silent ride home. No one mentioned the car part. No one had even looked for it. Certainly not Dad. He was clearly lying. What were we doing out there? It seemed inconceivable that Dad had kidnapped us once, but he had. But to kill his own children? Could he possibly be capable of it?

Chapter 8

In the second grade I had a teacher named Mrs. Hatch. She was tall and lanky and looked twenty years older than she was. Looking back now I think she was a smoker with all those wrinkles and that deep, gravelly voice. I would bet the farm.

Mrs. Hatch didn't like me for several reasons. For one thing, I refused to say the Pledge of Allegiance. It didn't feel right to me. Not to mention my new dad enlisted to serve his country and came back beaten up and vocal about what he thought of our government. Boycotting the Pledge made me feel like I was supporting him in my way. It was no secret the war had ruined my dad and my family. I had nothing to pledge.

Mrs. Hatch also thought I was ridiculous because of what happened one day when Daddy Frank came to pick me up from school.

"Get your stuff, Sparrow, we are going to get Happy Meals and then we're going to the toy store."

Did I just hear that correctly? I sprinted to the coat closet to collect my things when Mrs. Hatch said,

"You can't go, you have Brownies tonight."

"I quit Brownies" I replied, but Frank decided I should honor my commitment.

"Oh, I forgot about Brownies. Guess we'll have to go some other time, Sparrow." And with that he turned to leave. I was devastated. Not only was I going to miss out on junk food and toys but I was worried they would take the other kids and I'd be left out. It's not like we went to the toy store regularly by any means.

"No!" I shrieked as I hurled myself onto the ground and firmly wrapped my arms around Frank's legs. He tried to shake me off but only managed to break one leg free. I had a death grip on the other.

"Please!" I cried. I knew everyone was looking at me but I didn't care. Quiet little Sparrow had come undone. Frank might have been an alcoholic (thank God he kicked the heroin) but in some ways he was a good dad. He pried me off of his leg and managed to escape. Frank never gave into my princess moments. He always gently held me accountable.

A few months after second grade began, I noticed someone was stealing my lunch. Just the snacks at first, but later the whole lunch. I had this white, faux patent leather Holly Hobbie lunch box that I adored. I kept it in the coat closet with the other kids' lunchboxes. Every day I noticed something missing. I could see why someone would want to steal my lunch as I had the lunch of champions: Sno balls, Cheese Curls, Hostess Cup Cakes, Ring Dings, Devil Dogs... you get the picture. Mom wanted us kids to really enjoy our lunch. Either that or it was easy to get our snacks at the local convenience store along with her Virginia Slims.

At first I had no idea who was taking my prepackaged goodies until I noticed Susie-Lynn munching on what I had in my lovely lunchbox that day. She even offered to share with me when she caught me staring at her devouring a Devil Dog that was meant to be in *my* belly. I was onto her, but now I had to prove it. The next day I decided to keep my eyes peeled to see if I could catch that sneaky lunch thief. A few minutes before our snack time Susie-Lynn said she had to use the bathroom and left the classroom. I waited and waited and sure enough she stopped in the coat closet on the way back. I quietly got up to see what she was up to and I caught her red-handed. There she was with my lunchbox wide open stealing my precious junk food.

"You're stealing my lunch!" I yelled and I stuck my arm out and pointed to her like you see people do on television when they are accusing someone of murder. Mrs. Hatch came running in and yelled at both of us.

"What's going on in here?"

"Susie-Lynn is stealing my lunch." Poor little Susie-Q was caught off guard, still sitting there with my open lunch box. She must not have had any siblings or she would have had the good sense to close the box quickly and make up a story that blamed me. Mrs. Hatch ignored Susie and told me to put my lunchbox under her desk from now on. I was pissed. How come Susie-Lynn wasn't getting into trouble? I had to stand in the corner for an hour once for whispering to someone to borrow a pencil and this lunch thief gets off scot free? I wasn't having it. Not to mention I would look like the teacher's pet with my lunchbox under her desk. Could I be any more of an outsider?

This was one I couldn't let go. Day after day I plotted and schemed about how I was going to make her pay for what she did. Maybe no one ever told this girl you don't steal food from a scrappy, poor kid. Not without consequences, anyway.

So I waited. I waited about two months, which is like ten years to a seven year old. I had my plan for a while; I just needed the right situation to carry it out. Magically it all came together. We were outside at recess playing in the snow. It was cold and dreary and miserable. Susie-Lynn looked like a happy little piglet, though, off by herself making snow angels. I decided I was gonna get that little snow pig. I convinced a classmate named Haley to help me since I had learned to be quite persuasive when I needed to be. We both charged over to Susie at full force and tackled her, shoving handfuls of snow down her snug-fitting snowsuit. It wasn't easy because she really filled that thing out but we kept going. She screamed but I grabbed the back of her head and shoved her face in the snow. It's amazing how well snow muffles sound. This probably went on for about two minutes; the happiest two minutes of my second grade year. We stopped when we couldn't get any more snow in. Susie's face had turned beet red and the tears streaming down her face became little icicles. She had snot strings coming out of both nostrils that rested on her puffy upper lip. I was satisfied. "That's for stealing my lunch," was all I said as I walked away, feeling like Wonder Woman in a snowsuit.

Naturally, Susie-Lynn told the teacher and I got into trouble. Susie's mom had to come to school to bring her a change of clothes, which made me even happier. My Operation Make Susie Pay was a success. I had to spend the rest of the day in the corner which was perfect since no one could see me grinning from ear to ear. People in my life always seemed to get away with hurting me: my dad, mom, step-dad. No one was accountable for their actions until now. Even though Mrs. Hatch yelled at me for eons and was disappointed in me I knew deep down I had stood up for myself. The only way I knew how.

* * *

I was excited to start third grade because it was in a different school called the New Suncook School. It was at least twenty miles outside town, which meant I had to get up super early to get there on time. I was really hoping for a nicer teacher than Mrs. Hatch and I fully thought I deserved one too. Putting up with her for a whole year seemed like eternity and I was ready for a fresh new face. Unfortunately the universe had other plans.

Blanche Claybourn was another crusty old teacher who should have retired years before I encountered her. I'm not sure why she would have wanted to become a teacher in the first place. She had a perma-scowl which would definitely meet the criteria for today's definition of a resting bitch face. She had short, blonde hair that was parted way over to the side which left her with a feathered comb-over, much like something you'd see on a late 1960s housewife, or a member of Herman's Hermits. Plus, it was nearly the eighties now and someone should have told her. Mrs. Claybourn's teacher sweaters definitely added to the dated look, but what was most unnerving about her was that her head leaned to the left way too much and she consistently spittled every time she talked. I learned to take a few steps back when she was talking to me, especially when she was angry.

Mrs. Claybourn had plenty of reasons not to like me. For one thing I knew she could tell I was one of "those" kids; the kids whose clothes didn't match, whose hair was messy, and who had permanent dirt rings around their necks. I wish I was exaggerating about that last one but once when I was kicking and screaming because I didn't want to get into the bath tub Frank lifted me up to the bathroom mirror and showed me the dirt ring around my neck.

"Sparrow, you have to take a tub, you're filthy," he told me. I'm not sure why we always called it "taking a tub" when everyone else said bath but in any event I wanted no part of either. I hated getting my hair wet and then getting water in my ears and soap in my eyes. Mom should have nicknamed me "Kitty" not "Puppy" but I guess she didn't know at the time I was part feline.

On top of having a dirt ring, Mrs. Claybourn probably hated me for stinking up her class. More than once she asked me if I smoked. I told her my parents did and she said she could tell because I reeked of cigarettes. I couldn't smell it because I was so used to it but my teacher had an aversion to smoke which didn't help my cause. She had no choice but to put me in her advanced reading and math groups because of my intellect, but I could tell she wasn't happy about it.

I was definitely that kid whose dog ate her homework. Mom never once asked if I had any after school, so I rarely remembered to do it. Mrs. Claybourn never missed an opportunity to call me out in front of the class for not having it. She would sigh those deep, heavy sighs that let me know I was the most annoying person in her life. Why was I such an energy drain for her? I couldn't figure it out. Didn't she know what my life was like? Didn't she know that I already felt worthless? I couldn't decide which was worse, being totally ignored at home or being the bane of someone's existence at school. Over time I figured out it was the latter. Actually, it became a no-brainer.

Patsy Harrington was a dark-haired girl a few years older than me who went to my school. She lived pretty close by and I remember the school bus picking her up shortly after it came down our street. She was tall and thin with stringy hair and I remember thinking she had a horse face, as it was long and skinny too. I didn't pay much attention to her until she began to pick on me. Being several years younger I was an easy target, especially since I was tiny and rumpled. More like a *perfect* target.

She would start by making fun of my clothes and hair, and when I tried to ignore her she ramped it up. This didn't go on long because even though she was older and I was intimidated I was still pretty scrappy and I knew I had to stick up for myself. So one day as she was starting in on me I noticed a couple of *Letter People* books on the seat next to her. These were books I had used in the first grade to help with reading, even though I already knew how. Each book was a different letter and they were very rudimentary. *What's a fifth grader doing with* Letter People *books?* I wondered. Then it hit me. She couldn't read.

"Well at least *I* know how to read," I said. *Take that you brat!* I thought, feeling self-righteous. I could have called her horse-face or something worse but it wasn't my style. I'm not saying I was perfect because the day before I had gotten into trouble for zipping Mikey up in a suitcase and trying to throw him down the stairs into the basement, but he was my brother and it didn't count. I never picked on kids at school. I was shy, but always friendly and nice—

unless someone crossed a line. I never started it, but sometimes I finished it, which is how I felt when I delivered the reading zinger. Patsy told me to shut up but I could see she was visibly disturbed which let me know I won that round. Good for me.

Not long after class began Mrs. Claybourn got called into the hall. When she came back she asked me to step outside. She had that intense scowl on her face and I felt my heart pounding but I couldn't think of anything I had done so I was bewildered. In the hall she bent over, grabbed my tiny shoulders and started shaking me, scream-spitting in my face.

"How dare you make fun of someone who can't read!" she hollered. She was about an inch away from my face and not only was I getting quite a spit bath but my hair started blowing back as well. "Patsy's working hard on her reading and just because you're advanced it doesn't give you any right to pick on her!" I had never seen her quite this angry as her face was turning red and her eyes were wild with fury.

"She picked on me first..."

"I don't care! You never pick on someone's learning disability! Do you hear me?" She was still violently shaking me at this point and I felt my head lolling like a rag doll. Everything got fuzzy and I saw stars. When she finally stopped she abruptly turned and marched back into the classroom, slamming the door behind her. I don't recall how I made it back to my desk because Mrs. Claybourn had shaken me out of my own body, but somehow I was able to use my legs to walk back into the classroom and take my seat.

Getting through that day was brutal. The other kids had overheard Mrs. Claybourn screaming at me and at recess they wanted to know what I had done. I tried to explain my side. Some kids understood and some didn't but no one cared all that much. It would just be something that had to blow over. Or so I thought.

When I got home from school Mom said the teacher had called and explained how I was bullying a girl at school and that I needed to make amends. I explained to her what happened but Mrs. Claybourn had gotten to her first and she wasn't buying my story.

"Your teacher thinks you two should spend some time together after school," Mom said as she lit a cigarette. "It'll be good for you."

"Mom, she's awful to me. I'm not hanging out with her!"

"Well, her dad's on his way over here to pick you up. You need to apologize. I've always taught you kids to root for the underdog. Sounds like you need some help with that lesson."

I didn't know how to tell Mom I *was* the underdog. Every. Single. Day. I was the kid who reeked of smoke, had holes in her shoes and wore mismatched clothes a size too small. I was trying to root for the underdog— myself! Why wasn't anyone else rooting for me? Mom never saw my plight. Someone else always had it worse. Once I tried to tell Mom I needed a new Barbie because Mikey had sawed one of her legs off with a steak knife. Mom said how dare I discard poor Barbie because she only had one leg, and that people with special needs were just as important. She insisted I continue to play with hop-a-long Barbie and appreciate the fact that I had two legs, unlike Barbie who had to try and keep up with Ken hopping around in her uncomfortable stiletto. Barbie had a rough life.

When Patsy's dad came to the door I collapsed inside myself like the beginnings of a black hole. I felt small and dark. To be fair he was a kind, jovial fellow who probably thought I was some troubled kid and he was doing a good deed for me by forcing me to hang out with him and his horse-faced daughter so I could see what a real family was like. Lucky me.

We went over to Patsy's house and I just sat there, quiet. She didn't know what to do either, because she knew she had started the whole mess. I was polite to her parents, yet solemn. There was no way I was going to be her friend. Luckily I was only there for about an hour or so, but it definitely seemed a lot longer. When they dropped me off at the house I raced to the front door without stopping to say goodbye. I knew I would never put myself through that again. How can these people not realize how important justice is to me after everything I had been through in my short life? Just more validation that the only one looking out for me was me.

* * *

One thing about living in the middle of nowhere is that you get creative with outdoor play. Mikey, Punky and I spent countless hours outside building forts, lighting fires (Mikey), vandalizing (Mikey again), catching toads and turtles, you name it. My brother and his friends would have poop contests in the backyard to see who could lay the biggest brick. They would drop their drawers one by one and line up right next to each other. I don't recall who won but I do remember Mom bitching about her missing paper towels. More than once our dog Snoopy broke his chain and came and ate all the turds, then chased us around the yard as we ran screaming at the thought of Snoopy trying to lick us with his turd breath.

Daddy Frank hated cops, which he called "pigs," and for some reason they came to our house often so he had Snoopy chained up in the front yard not far from our front door. I always felt bad for Snoopy. He was large and intimidating, part German shepherd, part wolf. His fur was mostly black with a little brown mixed in and was thick as hell. He would have devoured anyone who came near him if not part of the family. He had a sad junkyard doghouse made of plywood that looked like it took exactly eight minutes to nail together. Snoopy was never walked or loved very much, so every once in a while he broke his chain and tore through the neighborhood and nearby woods. Mom always gave us a bag of deli ham and said, "Go catch Snoopy." We spent hours chasing after him and he always came home. I don't think it was for the ham. He loved us and was part of the family; he just needed his moments to run wild.

As much as we loved the outdoors we were addicted to Saturday morning cartoons. We had exactly two channels, three if you counted PBS (we didn't). We didn't watch much during the week but we were all about Saturday mornings. One Saturday we were sitting on the floor in front of our 19" color Zenith eating Fruity Pebbles and watching Bugs Bunny when there was a knock at the door. Mom was in the dining room smoking a cigarette and having her coffee. Frank had gone to the dump to either drop off trash or look for treasures. Mom went to the door and the man knocking stepped inside and explained he was with the rental place and was there to collect the television since no payments had been made. Mom was normally passive with strangers but I saw her face change and she looked angry.

"You mean to tell me you're gonna take this television away from my three kids?" Mom looked over at us and as if on cue we all started crying.

"Please, mister, don't take our TV!" I wailed. My brother went into one of his full-blown ear-piercing meltdowns which I now realize probably put him on the spectrum, though no one talked about that in those days. Even little Punky who couldn't have been more than three or four joined in. The repo-man looked devastated.

"Okay fine lady, keep your TV," he muttered as he turned and bolted out the door. I'm sure he sprinted past Snoopy. I'm shocked he even made it to the front door in the first place.

After he left we all cheered and high-fived. Mom seemed very pleased with herself and us. The one time she was glad we were all having tantrums. Normally, when one of us cried she would freak out and say "You kids are killing me!" But not this day. She was proud of her little monsters. Mom said she never heard back from the rental company. We were able to keep our 19" Zenith color TV.

Growing up poor didn't bother me much at first. I guess I didn't know the difference. I thought all kids got on their knees and prayed to Jesus for milk and eggs. I was a good little prayer too. I used to throw in requests for Lucky Charms, Orange Crush and anything else I could think of. Usually our prayers were answered. It wasn't until I got a little older that I realized Jesus always blessed Mom with cigarettes and Pepsi. Mom would sit at the dining room table puffing away and say, "Kids, go pray that the Lord brings us food this week." We used to kneel in front of that plastic-covered loveseat and pray our hungry little hearts out. I knew that if Jesus got Mom her smokes he wouldn't begrudge me milk and eggs.

Mom also got food from our church on occasion. Around the time I was eight or so Mom joined a local Evangelical church. It was fun at first. We went Sunday mornings, Sunday evenings and Wednesday evenings too. They had programs for kids, and we got to run around and play a lot. Our cars often broke down so more than once people came from the church to pick us up. I guess they really wanted to make sure we didn't miss out. Mom seemed to like all the attention. They doted on her at first but it didn't take long before they tried to change her. With her heavy makeup, painted fingernails, sleeveless tops, and cigarettes I think they saw her as a Jezebel in the flesh and a challenge to convert. I'm sure they saw us kids as heathens since we were wild and mouthy as ever.

One Sunday the pastor told us we had to bring in our secular music for a church burning. I was pissed. So was Frank. Mom made him bring in all of his Pink Floyd and Led Zeppelin albums. I had to bring my little 45 of Queen's "Another One Bites the Dust." That was a sad day. Unfortunately it didn't stop there. That same Sunday, Pastor Ken asked if anyone in the congregation was suffering from any afflictions that needed prayer. That happened often and usually there would be one or two parishioners who asked for redemption for their alcohol or cigarette addiction. The pastor asked them to come to the pulpit for hands-on prayer and deliverance. It wasn't at all uncommon to see them fall to the ground and convulse like they were having an epileptic seizure. The best part was when the pastor hovered over them holding a Bible in the air, speaking in some foreign language that Mom said was called tongues. When I asked more detailed questions she really couldn't answer except to say it was a holy language. I never comprehended what the point of a holy language was if we couldn't understand it.

One Sunday Mom dragged me to the pulpit because Pastor Ken told everyone who wanted the gift of tongues to come to the front. Mom must have thought since I asked so many questions I was a good candidate, so she had the associate pastor Lou pray over me. He prayed and prayed in his holy language with his hand on my head and it was awkward because he was waiting for me to speak this tongues language only I was secretly singing "Another One Bites the Dust" in my head. When I finally couldn't take the pressure anymore I made up my own holy language which was "Another One Bites the Dust" said backwards and everyone thought I was blessed with the spirit. I was so relieved to have him move onto the next victim that I didn't care that I had turned into a total fraud.

What was worse was that same day Pastor Ken kept calling out to the congregation that there was someone afflicted with a horrible addiction and that person should reveal himself to be saved. There was a hush that pervaded the room but that didn't stop Pastor Ken. "Come on, I know you're out there. Stop hiding," he said with conviction.

Out of nowhere my friend Terry's dad stood up.

"It's me, Pastor. I have a terrible addiction."

"What is it, son? How has Satan gotten a-hold of you?"

"I'm addicted to...Pac-Man!" Terry's dad said as he broke into sobs. I was shocked that Mr. Black would think playing Pac-Man was such a bad thing. I had played on more than one occasion and I thought it was fantastic. Pure genius, actually. I didn't see the problem or why Mr. Black had to create such drama. He eagerly went running to the front and Pastor Ken laid hands on him, eventually pushing him to the ground, so he could do that convulsing thing and burn off the calories he had consumed from eating that morning's church donuts. Poor Terry. He must have been mortified, but even worse; he would probably never get to play another game of Pac-Man ever again.

Mom really got into this religion thing. She had always talked about God before, here and there but now she was full-on obsessed with Jesus and the Bible, which is probably why she also became obsessed with televangelists. Every weekend when it was show time she got her coffee and cigarettes and nestled into the couch to watch Praise the Lord (PTL) with Jim and Tammy Faye Bakker. When Mom sat on the couch to watch TV we kids would all fight to see who would get Mom's leg. Mom would curl up on the armrest and bend her legs in underneath her so the side of her leg would be available. Mom had a very round ass and it made for a comfortable pillow, and sometimes she would play with our hair. Mikey and I would battle it out but we usually got equal time. Then little Punky would crawl somewhere in between which we never minded because she was tiny and cute and didn't make a peep. We cherished this time because it was the only time Mom was affectionate. Mom wasn't big on hugs anymore and often if we tried to hug her she would push us off and say, "Stop hanging on me!" But if the moon was in the seventh house and Jupiter was aligned with Mars she would let us cuddle up on her leg and not push us off. It was blissful.

In addition to PTL Mom also watched Jimmy Swaggart. Sometimes I would watch too and wonder why he yelled so loud and sweated so much. He would get so excited and flail his Bible in the air and soon the sweat beads on his forehead would start pouring down his face like an afternoon thundershower. He talked a lot about sin, and he scared me more than Jim Bakker, although Tammy Faye's eyelashes gave me nightmares, especially when she cried and the mascara ran down her face and made it look like she cried black tears just like Mom on the day she got me back. I think she and Mom shared makeup tips, and I was sure Tammy Faye used Mary Kay, just like Mom.

It wouldn't have been so bad if Mom just watched these shows for inspiration, but she also sent them money. She called the pledge line frequently and sent twenty dollars at a time on a fairly regular basis. I couldn't quite figure out why we were praying for food if Mom was sending Tammy Faye the twenty dollars that would buy us milk, eggs and Sno Balls. It just didn't make sense. Tammy was dressed so nice and wore lots of jewelry so how could she need our money? Not to mention she was always praying, so I'm sure Jesus kept her pantry stocked with all things Hostess.

* * *

After the whole *Letter People* incident things became more and more difficult for me at school. I didn't fit in with the other kids and felt like such an outsider. Even though I was in the advanced group I still didn't have many friends. I felt invisible.

One day I came up with a brilliant plan. I was standing outside waiting for the school bus and a sense of dread washed over me. I would rather be anywhere except at that weird-smelling school. On a whim I dove into the bushes when I heard the bus make the turn onto my street. I peeked through the branches and watched it pass by. I waited about five minutes until it went to the end of the street and passed back again, then when it was out of sight I strolled back in the house as if nothing was wrong. Mom was furious.

"Sparrow! Why didn't you get on the bus?" At first, I would come up with what I thought were clever excuses. "I forgot my lunch box" or "I had to pee." After a while I just laughed and ran around the living room as Mom chased me. Sometimes she caught me by the hair, wrapping it around her hand several times and pulling kind of hard at the base of my neck. I can't say I blame her. It was over thirty miles to school and she never took me because I think she was too afraid the car would break down.

One time she tried to hold me accountable and told Frank to take me. He was happy to oblige, but once we got in the car he said we had to make a pit stop. We stopped at his good friend George's house so they could have an early morning cold one. I sat on the couch watching TV as they drank and laughed and gossiped like women at the kitchen table. I kept asking when we were leaving. "In a minute, Sparrow, calm down," Frank said.

After several hours I decided to call Mom. "Mom, I'm at George's house and Frank's drinking."

"Put him on the phone," she said.

Frank never once got pissed at me, but he looked a bit defeated as he grabbed the phone. I could hear Mom yelling on the other end. She told him to bring my ass to school.

"Too bad, Sparrow, you could have had a day off," he said, slowly shaking his head. He reeked of beer but at age eight I was a pretty good judge of drunk people and I deemed him safe to drive. Funnily enough we never made it to school because a few miles down the road one of the wheels fell right off the car. I think it was the front left one. Back to George's house we went.

Chapter 9

During the spring of my ninth year Frank scored some extra money and went to the local department store to get us all bikes. Brand new bikes! This was a big deal because Frank had pretty much stopped working at this point. I still don't know if he quit or was fired from his jobs but I do know he was showing up to work reeking of booze. Frank's morning routine was to get up, drive down to the Little Mountain Store about a mile down the road, and buy two cans of Colt 45. He was able to hide a can in each Harley-Davidson motorcycle boot and when he came back into the house he went straight to the bathroom. I would hear the door lock, then I'd hear the first pop top. He must have downed the first beer quickly because I'd hear the second pop top not long after. Then he would open the window, throw the cans out, belch loudly, close the window and rejoin the family. He was ready to start the day.

He had brought Mikey to the local department store with him so Mikey got to pick out his own bike. Frank went ahead and chose Punky's bike and my bike too. When they got home Frank came into the house calling for Mom.

"Joanie, we gotta talk. Mikey insisted on a pink bike." Mom was surprised at first but didn't really see the harm in it. Frank persisted. "Joanie, I can't let him ride that bike up and down the block. He's gonna get the shit beat out of him." Mom insisted he'd be fine.

Frank tried to convince Mikey one more time to exchange the bike for a boy's BMX, but he was crazy about the pink Huffy. Frank got Punky a yellow bike with a huge banana seat and a decal that said "Country Sunshine" on the side. My bike was tan and dark brown and looked like a grownup's bike, so I was excited but also a little disappointed that the colors looked like something you would find in a litter box.

Frank put mine together last and I was ready to go. He didn't really own tools, so he used a butter knife. I was shocked at what you could accomplish with a little know-how and a butter knife and I took note. I didn't know how to ride a bike, but I was convinced I could ace it no sweat. I tried to get on but it was so big and heavy that every time I tried the bike and I fell over. Frank started laughing.

"Looks like this bike is pretty big. Here I'll help you." Frank set his beer down and held the bike steady so I could get on. Success! I sat on the seat but my feet didn't reach the pedals. "I can't adjust the seat any more Sparrow, it's already all the way down."

At first I felt deflated, but seeing my brother and sister getting comfortable on their bikes I was determined. Frank said he would help. I figured out I could pedal the bike as long as I was standing. And if Frank held onto the back and jogged beside me I was good.

It became obvious pretty quickly that Frank had never taught a kid how to ride a bike before. His idea of helping was to run alongside me then give a big push and let me fly solo. "It's the only way you'll learn, Sparrow."

The first few times I crashed and burned pretty fast. Even though I was on a women's three speed bicycle the bars can still attack you in your nether regions and cause intense pain. But I wasn't giving up. This was before helmets, knee pads and the like, so I was pretty scraped up from head to toe, but by the end of the day I knew how to ride that bike. I just had to ride standing up. My bike was ugly and too big but I owned it. I mastered that thing and made it mine.

Mikey, on the other hand, had second thoughts about his bike. After riding through our neighborhood a few times he came home and threw his Huffy down on the ground. "I hate this bike!" he wailed. It seems a few boys tore him to shreds about his pink Huffy.

"You picked it out, Mikey, you have to ride it," Frank had decided. Mikey ultimately embraced his bike and the boys in the neighborhood eventually stopped teasing him. I even caught a few of them riding it from time to time. I, on the other hand, never touched that pink bike. It was too girly and riding it seemed too easy.

* * *

School continued to get worse and worse. At home I was comfortable being me. I was also one of the oldest kids on the block, so I was the ringleader. But school was a different story. I was a year younger than everyone else and still painfully shy. I didn't feel like I belonged.

Mom didn't help me get ready in the mornings and I began noticing the other girls at school had clothes that weren't stained or wrinkled, and their hair always looked nice with braids, pony tails, and fancy barrettes. One girl always had little alligators on her shirts. She wore plaid skirts with knee socks and never once did I see a hair out of place. In fifth grade she sat a few seats up from me in the row to my left and I would catch myself staring at her. Kristen Harris. Never had I ever wanted to be anyone in my life but I wanted to be her.

On top of being perfect Kristen was also beautiful, with long, bleach-blonde hair, and a darker complexion that reminded me of Malibu Barbie. Her teeth were so white I think they glowed in the dark. She smiled a lot so I always got to admire them. Mine were still growing in and had a giant space in between them but hers didn't. She had the teeth of a twenty-five-year-old Crest model.

Kristen had a boyfriend named Justin Shaw. He had the same bleach blond hair and darker complexion. They easily could have passed for brother and sister. Justin also had little alligators on his shirts. He never talked to me except to say, "Here comes gorilla arms" when I approached the playground at recess. There was no hiding my Italian heritage with those arms. Funny I had never really noticed how hairy they were until Justin pointed them out to myself and everyone in the fifth grade. I was elated when he moved away later that year. Not only did the teasing stop but it was kind of nice to see everyone's favorite couple broken up.

To be fair Mom didn't have a lot of time to tend to three unruly children. She and Frank had separated, and he moved out of the house. She said his drinking just got to be too much, and he was no longer able to work. At first I was bummed because we had tried so hard to get him to stop. All those trips to the VA hospital where he agreed to go for treatment were in vain. Mom always drove with Frank in the front and us kids in the backseat.

"Bye Daddy! Please stop drinking!" we yelled out of the car window as he shuffled into the hospital carrying a crumpled paper bag I assumed had a change of clothes in it. This happened countless times and each time we were convinced it would be the last. Unfortunately he only stayed long enough to dry out and would show up back at the house after a few days, like an unwanted dog that finds its way home after being dropped off at a farm miles away. Mom always seemed surprised, but then he would tell her he hitch-hiked back because he didn't want to put her out. The reality was he didn't want her to fight him about leaving. He stayed sober a total of three days or so before he was back to beer for breakfast.

Frank wasn't the type of person who was going to sit in a circle and tell strangers his problems. What would he say? That he saw kids get blown to bits in Vietnam? That his platoon was annihilated, he saw his good friends get their faces blown off, and that he was walking around with shrapnel in his chest? It wasn't his style. Mom told me that he was so disgusted with the war he threw his medals in the trash and she had to dig them out. Two bronze stars and a purple heart. He said they meant nothing to him and he wanted no vestige of his time there. But he couldn't forget, at least not without a beer in each boot. So she finally had to ask him to leave.

As sad as it sounds things weren't that much different after Frank left. He had become fairly unreliable due to his drinking, so we saw him more as a fixture than a dad. He was passing out drunk more and more, and we couldn't wake him up. He would lie on the couch and you could scream in his ear and punch him hard yet nothing worked. He was out. Several times I thought he was dead because his face was gray and it seemed like he wasn't breathing. But in time I quit worrying and graduated to drawing on his face with a Sharpie, giving him makeovers with Mom's Mary Kay and once I opened his eyelid and studied the human eyeball for a good twenty minutes. I discovered eyes are very spongy and slimy.

There was no fighting or bitterness when he left, just goodbyes. He had a few tears as he hugged each of us. When it was my turn he hugged me tight and I nestled my face in his long hair. He smelled like beer and cigarettes. I was sad for a moment but as soon as he left I convinced myself it was for the best. I decided I needed a dad who could pay the electric bill.

One downside for Mom when Frank left was that it was harder for her to get Mikey and me to behave. Mikey was always getting into trouble in the neighborhood. When our neighbors went out of town he took a garden hose and stuck it in the window of their bedroom and turned on the faucet full force. When the Brown's returned they had one flooded house on their hands. Not long after he lit a fire in an open lot across the street. Luckily the neighbors put it out before it got too out of hand. Somehow he always got away with that kind of thing.

I never vandalized other people's property but shortly after Frank left I decided to take up smoking. Up to this point I was so mad at Mom for smoking that I often took her cigarettes out of the pack, broke them in half, and put them back in the pack so when she went to take one out she found them all broken and unsmokable.

"Sparrow!" she yelled. "Leave my cigarettes alone!" Then she painstakingly tried to put them back together with Scotch tape.

One day I happened to notice Mom all stressed out go over to the kitchen table, pick up her cigarettes, and take one out of the pack. She was smoking Merits at the time and the pack was white with a yellow emblem. I had watched Mom smoke a million times before but this time was different. I noticed how Mom's face totally relaxed after taking just one drag. She exhaled and looked so peaceful—she was even smiling a little. I wondered why I hadn't tried this smoking thing again earlier. It sure seemed like the answer to everyone's problems. All four of my parents smoked. (I was forced to smoke once when I was five but that was different and I was a baby back then.)

I decided I needed to see what all the fuss was about. When Mom left the kitchen I took a cigarette out of the pack and grabbed the book of matches on the table. I slipped into the bathroom and locked the door. I gently opened the window all the way to help with the smell. I put the cigarette in my mouth just like Mom did and plucked a match out. I had watched my parents use matches lots of times so I felt like a pro. I struck the match and it lit on the first try. I brought it to the end of the cigarette and took a deep breath in just like Mom did. I even closed my eyes to try to get the same effect.

I wasn't prepared for what happened next. I began coughing uncontrollably and couldn't stop. I remembered that happening the first time I smoked but I thought it was because I was only five and just not ready. At nearly ten I l felt like I should have been able to handle it. But I was wrong. Once I stopped coughing I decided to take another puff and figured out how to smoke without actually inhaling. I felt so grown up, so free. I puffed and puffed and even looked in the mirror as I was sucking in. I watched the end of the cigarette glow really brightly, then get dimmer as I stopped puffing. I even felt like a grownup flicking the ashes into the sink. I was curious to know how people knew exactly when it was time to flick the ashes. I wanted to do it just right, so I experimented.

Mom caught on. I think she heard me coughing and I'm sure she smelled the smoke. She banged on the bathroom door. "Sparrow! What are you doing in there? Are you smoking? Come out of there right now!"

I completely ignored her. I wasn't afraid of her at all, plus I was in smoke heaven in that tiny little bathroom. By this point I had also started digging into Mom's Mary Kay collection and was contemplating giving myself a makeover. Mom always had the coolest makeup, and she painted her face every day with thick, black eyeliner and gobs of mascara and almost always a nude lip. Since I was now a smoker like Mom, I thought I should also look the part. But Mom wouldn't stop beating on the door. She killed my Merit high and I let her in after holding my cigarette under the running faucet to put it out. She tried to yell at me but I walked away. I had found a new readily accessible toy that I didn't have to beg my real dad or Jesus for. I was happy.

It didn't take Mom long after Frank left to start dating. Who could blame her? With her looks I'm sure she was asked out quite a bit. She would get a babysitter on occasion and then sometimes invite her dates in for coffee when she got home. I remember two guys in particular: Ralph and another man named Frank. Ralph was an attractive artist who lived in a chalet on a nearby lake. His hair was prematurely gray and he had piercing blue eyes. Mom seemed smitten. She brought me over to his house once and he had several small plants in his loft growing under heat lamps.

"Nice tomato plants" Mom said to Ralph, in a teasing manner.

"Those are pot plants, Mom."

"They are not, Sparrow!" I knew they were because I recognized the smell. Dad and his second wife Samantha smoked pot regularly at night, at least when I was there visiting which was every summer and school holidays. They locked themselves in their bedroom and smoked while watching Johnny Carson. They laughed hysterically and I heard everything since my room was right next to theirs. My older stepsisters were the ones who told me what it was. Sometimes we knocked on their door if we needed something but once they were high they would never answer. We were on our own.

Mom and Ralph didn't last long. I'm not sure why. He did seem a little overwhelmed by the fact that Mom had three "active" children. Maybe he just couldn't deal, especially since he didn't have any kids of his own. She quickly moved on to her next love interest, Frank number two. He was tall with short, dark hair and a thick, untrimmed mustache. I only remember him coming over a couple of times.

The first time Mom had him over for dinner she put us kids to bed early. There was no way I was missing out on her date, so I crept down the hall when they were in the kitchen making coffee and wedged myself between the couch and the wall. I was tiny and could easily fit if I lay with my back against the wall, like a human piece of paper. It was tight but I didn't care. By age ten I didn't have faith in Mom's ability to choose a man, and if this guy was going to be the new daddy I wanted to know all about him. They made their way into the living room and were making small talk when Frank said, "Joan, I have something to tell you."

"Yes?" Mom replied as she sipped her coffee.

"Joan, I have herpes." Mom spit out her coffee and I imagined it spraying all over.

"Oh, my. Well, thank you for telling me," she said.

"Uh...I haven't had an outbreak in a really long time, but I thought you should know."

I had no idea what herpes was but I kind of knew what an outbreak was and I knew it was bad. Once there was an outbreak of chicken pox at school and half my class was missing for a week. *What the hell is herpes?* I couldn't wait to find out. We had a few encyclopedias Mom got with some green stamps from the IGA food store but I couldn't recall at that moment if we had H. Mom had stopped getting encyclopedias because we needed a new suitcase, so we didn't have the entire set.

Mom and lover boy talked for a long time. I fell fast asleep. I woke up in the middle of the night and at first was a little scared, not knowing where I was. Then I remembered I was still wedged behind the sofa. I worked my way out and tiptoed into my sister's room. Sometimes if I woke in the middle of the night I got scared and would drag either my brother or sister down the hall to sleep in my bed with me. Rarely, I would climb in bed with one of them. They had bunk beds and shared a room that always smelled funny because our cat Marsha would leave giant, foamy loads of diarrhea under the bottom bunk. The whole ensemble was too heavy for any of us to lift once Frank had left so no one could get to the piles to clean them up. I always kept the door to my room closed because I hated the smell of poop and I didn't want animals in there.

The next morning Mom was in a pretty good mood, but she looked strange. She had a red ring around her mouth and the skin around her lips was dry and cracked. I asked what was wrong with her face.

"Frank and I did some kissing last night and my lips got chapped."

I had seen people kiss before but I had never seen that. I even had a make out session with my sometimes boyfriend George once but I ended up punching him in the face because he tried to stick his tongue down my throat and that was the most disgusting thing I could think of other than eating worms.

"That's how people kiss," he insisted.

"Not this girl."

Mom looked like she had been making out with a St. Bernard all evening.

Chapter 10

Part of Mom and Dad's agreement was that Mikey and I spent summers with Dad. I dreaded going to Dad's because for one thing it was boring. He lived in a new place every year so it was nearly impossible to make friends. And he lived in the Deep South, which meant the summers were sweltering. My little body was used to the much colder New England climate so playing outside in Alabama heat was unbearable.

Dad's new wife Samantha was nice enough but she was a true southern belle who kept a perfect house and who wanted us to be perfect at all times. Sometimes she worked but mostly she stayed at home and was in charge of us during the day. She said it was unacceptable to be in the house all day so she would kick us outside and lock the door. We could either walk to the local pool, which we did a lot, or we could play in the yard, which really meant find some shade and count the hours.

Sometimes she let me stay inside if I played the piano, which I learned to love. Samantha and Dad had a piano because her two daughters took lessons. Carla and Pamela were three and five years older than me, respectively. Despite the lessons neither girl loved playing. I asked for lessons too but Dad said he wasn't going to waste the money since I was only there for the summer. Undeterred I studied their books, asked them certain questions that puzzled me such as what 2/4 was or what pp meant, and just taught myself. I learned a skill and I kept myself from melting in the Alabama heat—a win-win.

My stepsisters were nice for the most part, except that they were the reason I smoked cigarettes for the first time. I coughed and hacked forever and thought I was going to die and then it got even worse because somehow Dad found out and put cigarettes on my plate for dinner that night and told me if I wanted to smoke I had to eat them too. I cried, devastated, and luckily he was just making a point so I didn't have to eat them after all. But it was enough to scare me away from smoking again, at least for a few more years.

The other reason I dreaded going to Dad's was because he missed his true calling as a surgeon. If you had any kind of ailment Dad wanted to operate on you with his pocket knife. Dad wasn't the kind to hug or console you if you had gotten hurt—he looked for ways to cut you open. The first time I found out about Dad's missed calling was when I showed him a wart on my thumb. It was right on the cuticle and no surprise I had gotten one because Charlie McLaughlin had a giant one on his index finger and rubbed it on my thumb one day in class, telling me that I would now have one too. He was right.

I innocently showed my wart to Dad because I needed it gone. I thought perhaps he would take me to the local pharmacy to get some medicine called Compound W. I had seen several commercials about that stuff and it looked like it worked miracles on peoples' unsightly finger fungus. Dad had other ideas. "Hold still," he murmured as he held my thumb with one hand and eased his pocket knife out of his pants with the other. Before I could blink he had gouged my little thumb with the blade and sliced the wart clean off. There was a huge hole left and blood gushed out of it. "Go get a paper towel," Dad said as he turned to go back to the television, wiping his knife on his pants before closing it up and putting it back in his pocket. I stood there, stunned. I didn't even have time to whimper, let alone cry out. I went and grabbed the paper towel and held it on my thumb for a long time. It kept bleeding and when I asked for a Band-Aid Dad's response was, "You're fine." He wasn't about to get out of his Barcalounger again for something so silly.

Dad performed another outpatient surgery on me one time when I had a stye on my eyelid. It was swollen and painful and I had no plans of calling any attention to it; however, Dad couldn't help but notice it.

"Come here, let me look at that," he ordered one night after dinner. I was reticent but not quite so fearful this time. After all, I was pretty sure Dad wasn't going to gouge my eye out with his pocket knife so I was relatively safe, I thought.

"Stay here," he told me as he disappeared into the living room. I had no idea what Dad was doing but my heart raced when I saw what he had in his hands when he returned—a gargantuan set of tweezers. Dad kept a grooming kit in the end-table drawer next to his favorite chair so he could pick his feet while he was watching golf or the races on TV. Dad was prone to ingrown toenails and he insisted that he needed to dig them out regularly instead of spending money to have the doctor take care of it. I had seen Dad go to town digging trenches on the sides of his big toes with those tweezers. What in the world was he going to do to me?

"Hold still," Dad said as he tilted my head back and studied my eye. "I know how to handle this. Don't move." Dad held my eye open with his thumb and index finger and grabbed more than a few of my eyelashes with the tweezers. This time I couldn't have blinked if I wanted to before he yanked with the brute force of a determined Viking. Once again I was too shocked to utter a sound; however I can assure you that experience hurt a thousand times more than the attack on my wart. This time it was my eyelid that was gushing blood and I didn't quite know what to do about it, but I instinctively forwent the paper towel and booked it to the bathroom where I locked myself in and grabbed a washcloth, wetting it before I held it up to my eye. I told myself the man was nuts and I must never let him come at me with metal appliances ever again.

I did not fit in with my southern family. They told me nonstop that I talked funny and called me Yankee on a daily basis, as if being a New Englander was a sin. They hated how I said soda instead of coke and they had to ask what sneakers were because they had only ever heard them referred to as tennis shoes. I despised fried okra and yearned for my Devil Dogs and cream cheese and jelly sandwiches. My stepmother Samantha cooked a traditional southern meal every night. Sometimes it was good. I loved her barbecued chicken, lima beans and mashed potatoes. I learned to appreciate her black eyed peas and corn casserole. I just couldn't deal with the salmon croquettes. Salmon in a can is perhaps the worst idea of the twentieth century. She mashed the salmon into patties with bread crumbs and huge chunks of onion and fried them up. They stank up the house for days on end and the smell made my stomach turn.

Every morning I asked Samantha what we were having for dinner so I knew if I should be full of dread all day or not. I tried to mask the taste and smell with gobs of ketchup, but to no avail. Nothing took away the dirty, rotten fish taste. I also tried to pick out the onions but would invariably miss a few which would instantly cue my gag reflex when they hit the back of my throat. I heaved through many dinners. Mikey was even worse and would gag and spit his food right onto his plate. He always caused the drama. I was more of a quiet protestor.

Making the transition every summer was tough in many ways. Living with Mom was a true free-for-all. Our house was almost always a disaster, we didn't bathe regularly, and could pretty much do what we wanted as long as we didn't disturb Mom's coffee and cigarette time, which was most of the time. Once I had dropped a toy in between the couch cushions so I decided to lift one up to search for it. By this time Mom had taken the plastic off the furniture which made it slightly more comfortable and worn. When I lifted the cushion I froze. There were hundreds of tiny little yellow worms wiggling around everywhere.

"Mom!" I screamed "Mom come here!" I was used to messes. I even had lice once. But this was truly alarming.

"What is it, Sparrow?" Mom was annoyed at having to get up from the table and leave her cigarette. I had no words so I just pointed, still holding the couch cushion. "Oh, those are just maggots," Mom said so casually you would have thought they were jellybeans. "Go get the vacuum." I did as I was told and when I came back she showed me how to use the extended hose piece and suck those little maggots right up.

"Like this," she said as she slowly moved the hose back and forth. By this time she had taken all three cushions off and the maggots had taken over. They were sucked up rather easily and made a noise that I still can't quite describe as they were ascending to their demise. I stood back, watching the whole thing, feeling faint.

"See, all gone. No big deal." Mom left the vacuum in the middle of the living room and went back to her cigarette. It was shocking since Mom would go into an all-out panic and scream fest if a wasp or hornet got into the house, yet she was completely unfazed by the most disgusting, squirmy critters that turn into equally disgusting flies.

Being at Dad's couldn't have been a more opposite experience. Everything was perfectly sterile and in its place. No wonder Samantha scrubbed us down as soon as we got there. After we were squeaky clean she went through our suitcases and made various faces of disgust as she held up each holey, stained article of clothing.

"Where are all the clothes we bought you for Christmas?" Samantha asked. I had no idea, as Mom would just stuff clothes in the blue IGA green stamp suitcase with the broken handle and who knew if they were even clean? "Well, Jeff, we're gonna have to take them shopping," she said to my dad, disappointed.

I always felt like such a burden. Dad lived in really nice homes with luxury cars and top of the line furniture and yet they always talked about how they didn't have any money. I never understood how that worked. They never had me pray for food so I thought they were rich and I felt like their surroundings were way too nice for me. It was as if I was Annie and they were renting me for the summer out of charity only I couldn't wait to go back to the orphanage where I could at least be my dirty little self and stand on my bed (with shoes on) and belt out "It's a Hard Knock Life."

During one of these summer visits when Mikey and I were away Mom began dating husband number three. Larry Watson. Mom had taken a job cutting hair at the salon inside the tennis club. It was called Mixed Doubles and she worked there to pay the bills while she was taking a few classes at the University of Maine in Portland. It was there she met Larry. He was a hair client who also played racquetball at the club. He didn't have much hair, however. He had what looked like a crown of brown, wavy, Brillo-like tufts that circled his head, but in the middle was a giant bald spot. The hair crown was a perfect potential bird's nest and that bald spot could have easily housed two birds and some eggs. I wondered if any had ever tried to land on him.

Divorced, a pilot, and only one kid—he must have seemed like a dream to her. It also helped that he was completely enamored of her looks. And to be fair he probably fell in love with her before he got to know her little heathens. She knew how to suck him in. Little

Punky was a quiet charmer. If there was ever a case of bait and switch...

It didn't take long before we started having sleepovers at Larry's house. Mom must have been trying hard to impress him because she started cleaning our house on a regular basis in case he decided to drop by unexpectedly. At first he won us with his outdoorsy side, taking us hiking, snowmobiling and so on. He may have even gotten us our first Atari if I'm not mistaken, which wasn't a bad idea if you wanted to keep four kids occupied.

Larry didn't cook much but he liked to show off and so he had us over for dinner a few times. The first time he made a ham and tried to make it look all fancy by putting canned pineapple, maraschino cherries and cloves on top. It looked and tasted delicious. We didn't get much meat at Mom's house so I took advantage and cleaned my plate. Mom left a few bites on hers and Larry was quick to comment.

"Joan, you need to clean your plate."

"What?" she asked as if she hadn't heard him correctly. He repeated himself, a little firmer.

"Clean your plate."

Mom looked bewildered, then defeated as she picked up her fork and choked down her last few bites. I took note of this, having already deemed myself Mom's protector. I didn't like how I was feeling. Later when I brought it up to Mom she brushed it off.

"He just didn't want me to waste the food he went to so much trouble to make," she said. I saw the look on her face and knew she was full of it. She looked just as scared as I felt.

It wasn't long after that Larry asked Mom to move in and she agreed. I didn't have a good feeling about it on several levels. I'd be leaving my friends and status in the neighborhood. I'd no longer have my own room, and Larry's daughter Katie was a tattletale who was always whining.

Katie and Mikey would go back and forth between fighting and kissing but mostly it was Mikey torturing her with pranks and relentless teasing. He was famous for putting his finger in her face and chanting, "I'm not touching you!" He also had a fascination with earlobes which he renamed "chubs" and constantly pulled on her ears when she wasn't looking while calling her frizz ball over and over because she had coarse, wavy hair. He could be such a turd.

I was ten by this point and had just finished the fifth grade. It wasn't a strong finish. We ended the year with a dance. I'm not sure whose idea it was to organize a dance for kids so young but someone must have thought it was a fine idea. I would have skipped it altogether except our class got out early so we could all dance before the school bus came. I had no choice.

The dance was in our gymnasium. For some reason there was a circle of chairs right in the middle of the gym. I didn't see a DJ so I wasn't sure where the music was coming from. They weren't playing anything good like my Andy or Led Zeppelin but I wouldn't have felt any more comfortable if they were. I took a seat in one of the chairs while everyone else was dancing. Everyone except me and Susie-Lynn. She and I had never interacted since the day I pummeled her with snow even though we had been in the same class each year. We sat and watched as everyone else was coupled up and having a good time. *At least I'm not sitting here alone*, I thought, feeling slightly relieved. Just as I exhaled a nerdy boy named Shawn came up and asked Susie-Lynn to dance. He was short and stocky with coke bottle glasses and a terrible hair cut but he saw something in Susie and she saw something in him. They both beamed as she stood up and he led her onto the dance floor.

There I sat, alone, on display in the middle of the room. The only girl in class that didn't get asked to dance. And I was a good dancer!

It would have been less traumatic if the chairs had been placed off to the side, so at least I could have made a good wallflower. But I was directly in the middle of the room, not even sure where I should direct my eyes because I knew it was impolite to stare and I was too embarrassed to make eye contact with anyone. I ended up staring at the ground, at my shoes, praying it would all be over soon.

* * *

I would begin sixth grade in a new school, which was another thing to dread. The new kid yet again. I felt like I had been through enough and even though I didn't click with my fellow classmates at least I knew them and they knew me and there was an odd level of comfort there, even if none of the boys wanted to dance with me. *Probably the gorilla arms*, I decided, since I had not figured out how to deal with that dilemma.

Moving into Larry's wasn't as bad as I thought it would be, at least not at first. I loved my new school and had the best sixth grade teacher on Earth, Mrs. Farrar. She was the kindest, most loving woman I'd ever met and I was blessed to call her my teacher. She took a special interest in me, perhaps because I was dedicated to my studies, or perhaps because she could tell I was attention-starved. By then I had discovered makeup and could fit into my mother's high heels, which I frequently wore to school. I had spent the summer trying to perfect my look, especially after the school dance fiasco the year before. I was determined not to start at a new school without looking my best. I had convinced Dad and Samantha to buy me some new school clothes and I was making a change. I had even gotten rid of that dirt ring, once and for all.

I must have done a decent job because that year the boys took notice. I had boyfriend after boyfriend and was even elected class vice-president. Was this really happening? And I had friends! Kids called and invited me to parties and to hang out at their houses. My whole life had turned on a dime. Gone were the days of hiding from the bus in the bushes. Now you couldn't pay me to miss a day of school.

Larry's house was a lot nicer than what I was used to and he kept it pretty clean. It did have rust-colored shag carpet in the living room that took an hour to vacuum because it was so old but there weren't clothes and toys and old food wrappers strewn everywhere (yet) so I was happy. He had a great big yard and we even had our own gas pump right in the front yard to the left of the garage. Airplane fuel. To this day I have no idea why he would install a gas pump at the house when we lived at least ten miles from the airport where he stored his plane. Sometimes he and Mom would gas up the cars with airplane fuel and would then comment on how much faster the cars would drive. Mom drove a silver station wagon that actually ran well because Larry helped her buy it and he drove a rusty, old, burgundy Chevy Blazer my brother nicknamed the Rust Puppy.

Larry would get angry at Mikey because any time we were going somewhere he would say, "Are we taking the Rust Puppy?" Then he would do that Aspergery thing where he would repeat it upwards of twenty-five times. "*Rust* Puppy. Rust. *Puppy. Rust.* Rust Puppy!" Each time he said it his inflection changed and he got progressively louder.

"Stop calling my car a rust puppy!" Larry would tell him. But that never worked with Mikey. He would just keep going. We would all be in the car and five minutes down the road my brother would still be saying Rust Puppy. When it finally got old for him he would switch to saying, "Chub!" and start pulling on Larry's earlobes from the backseat. Thank God for my Walkman.

It was in the sixth grade that I developed my first crush on a boy my age and in my class. Conrad Darby had shaggy blond hair, ocean blue eyes and a chin that had such a deep groove it almost looked like it was cut in half. Kind of like a chin butt. But I loved it and tried to catch glimpses of it in class when he wasn't looking.

Conrad was my first real boyfriend. I used to ride my bike over to his grandmother's house since she lived up the street from me and he often went there after school. We sat outside on the stoop and hung out. He was kind of shy so many times we would sit in silence but it was still wonderful. Not once did he ever invite me inside. I'd heard through the grapevine that his grandmother was a hoarder and the house was a disaster so maybe he was too embarrassed. Whatever the case, it wouldn't have mattered to me since I could be quite at home in the midst of a mess.

One day I rode my bike over and Conrad was waiting outside with his boom box. As I sat down he said, "I got a new cassette and I want you to hear this song." I could see he had a copy of Prince's *Purple Rain* and decided to play his favorite song, "Darling Nikki." The first line was about a girl named Nikki who was a sex fiend. I became very uncomfortable and my face got really hot. *Why is he playing this? This is so embarrassing!* The song went on to describe how Nikki masturbated with a magazine. Conrad stopped the cassette player. "Do you know what that means?"

"Yes," I said, barely audible. He pushed play again and let the song finish. Suddenly it became really difficult to stare at his chin butt, so I looked away. After the song was over neither of us spoke. I had been dying for Conrad to hold my hand, maybe brush his leg up against mine, but I certainly wasn't ready to discuss anything remotely related to sex. We had ever even touched. Was he trying to tell me something?

I knew what the song meant because I had discovered lots of things about sex after we had moved into Larry's house. He owned a copy of *The Joy of Sex* which I had already read cover to cover. I didn't understand most of it so I concentrated on the drawings which were disgusting because the women were drawn with copious amounts of armpit hair and I couldn't imagine people would find that attractive. He also had some pretty dirty porno mags that he had gotten overseas. (I assume he had gotten them overseas because they were not in English). They were way more graphic than the *Playboy* and *Hustler* magazines my dad used to keep in his downstairs bathroom.

Dad had this big, brown ceramic planter-looking thing that he kept all his magazines in. I soon discovered the boring *Field & Stream* mags were on the outside and the naughty ones were conveniently tucked in the middle. Since it always took me what seemed like hours to make I would sit and read Dad's dirty collection. I knew I'd probably get in trouble, but I was curious and couldn't help myself. One time I came across a *Penthouse* centerfold that had a circle around the model's vagina with writing that said "scratch and sniff." I scratched and scratched but could not sniff anything; there was no scent. *Must be a defect,* I thought since I had a whole collection of scratch and sniff stickers and every one of them worked just fine. Strawberry, lemonade, I even had one that smelled like a martini. I was bummed I'd never know what vagina smelled like.

* * *

Mom and Larry decided to get married that year during our spring break. Larry proposed to Mom with an emerald and diamond ring that Mom was proud to show off. I begged her not to do it since the newness had worn off and Larry proved to have quite a temper. He quickly went from the fun guy who took us snowmobiling and hiking to the guy who gave us an endless list of chores and barked orders. He had no tolerance for noise or fighting

and yelled and screamed if we got on his nerves, which was daily.
Mom insisted God himself told her to marry him. For a quick
second I believed her, then instantly realized she was mistaken. I
knew in my soul God wouldn't want me to have Larry as a dad and
so I decided that Mom's misunderstanding would not make me
hate God or Jesus, for that matter. It was obvious Mom just needed
to have her hearing checked.

They decided to jet off to Reno without the rest of us and asked
Larry's brother Doug to watch us for the week. Punky was staying
with Mom's best friend Peg and Mikey was off visiting Dad so it
was just Katie and me at the house.

Doug was twenty-five and seemed like a fun guy. He was tall,
kind of heavy, with straight, dark brown hair and a round face. His
teeth were yellow and crooked and he had a double chin. When he
smiled he reminded me of the Cheshire cat. No one in her right
mind would have called him attractive. He was always laughing
and joking, which was a large part of his charm.

At first things were fine. Fun, even. Katie and I were making up
dance routines to the Go Go's and lip syncing into our hair brushes.
It was fun to be off of school for a week even though I missed my
friends. Then things started to change.

One afternoon a few days after Mom and Larry left, Doug
informed us that we needed to go to the landfill. There was no trash
service of any kind back in those days, so we stored our trash in the
garage and about once a month loaded it up and took it to the local
dump. On this day we loaded the garbage bags into the back of the
Rust Puppy and off we went. I was riding in the front and Katie
was in the back seat. As we were driving I felt eyes on me. He kept
looking over at me and smiling really big. I got an uncomfortable
feeling and looked away, but his eyes were boring holes in me and I
felt uneasy. My spidey sense kicked in but I didn't understand why.
I didn't feel like I was in danger like I did with Dad that day in the
swamp. I was fairly certain Doug didn't have a gun. What was this

about? I acted nonchalant but I didn't let my guard down. I kept searching the recesses of my mind to figure out what this feeling was. Then it hit me. He is looking at me like how Sylvester looks at Tweety. Like he wants to eat me. But that didn't make any sense. Why would he look at me that way? I was at a loss. I knew I wasn't safe but I had never had anyone look at me like that so I was puzzled. *Stay alert,* my mind told me.

Later that day I was hanging out on the couch coloring when I heard a voice from my room.

"Sparrow, come in here. Come lie down with me." Doug had decided to take a nap in my bed. I had a queen-size bed I shared with Punky and he was in it calling for me.

"No thanks" I replied, feeling even more uncomfortable. At that point I was hoping that if I ignored him it would stop. I kept coloring.

Shortly after he came out of the room and joined me on the couch. I went on coloring and was ignoring him when he started tickling me. "Stop!" I cried but it was no use. He climbed on top of me and was laughing up a storm as his hands were wandering all over my body. He was cleverly feeling me up under the guise of tickling me. "Get off me!" I screamed but he kept on. His hands quickly made their way up my shirt. I screamed. I fought and fought but he was too heavy for me. He felt like dead weight on my tiny frame.

Katie heard my screams and came running in to see what was going on. She saw me squirming and I saw the look on her face go from confusion to fierceness. Within a second she had jumped on Doug's back and started beating him in the head with her tiny, eight-year-old fists. I had never seen the little crybaby act so tough.

"Get off me!" Doug yelled but Katie kept pounding away. In order to get her off he had to take his hands off me. As he got up I sprinted out of the living room, out the back door and went running for my life to the house behind us. My friend Shelly lived there and I prayed she was home. I pounded on the back door with both fists and she quickly answered.

"What's going on? Are you okay?" she asked.

"No, I'm not. You need to hide me."

"Get in here," she said as she put me in a little broom closet in the kitchen.

"Where's your mom?"

"She's in the salon cutting hair. Don't worry, she doesn't know you're here."

Shelly's mom Betty had a hair salon attached to the house and she was busy cutting someone's hair. She was nice but I didn't trust her to protect me since she had dated Larry once and got along great with Doug. I was glad she didn't know I was there.

It didn't take five minutes for Doug to come looking for me. I was still panting in the closet when I heard a knock at the back door. Shelly answered.

"Is your mom here?" he asked.

"I'll go get her," Shelly said. I could see him through the crack between the door and the frame. He was looking around the house seeing if he could catch a glimpse of me. I wondered if he could hear my heart beating out of my chest.

"Hi Doug," Betty said as she wiped her hands on her apron. "What's going on?"

"Oh, I was just wondering if Sparrow was over here playing."

"No, I haven't seen her." *Oh thank God. She doesn't know I'm here.*

"Huh, I could've sworn she came over here."

"I'll keep you posted if I see her," Betty told him. He stood there for what seemed like forever before he finally turned and left.

Betty went back to her salon and Shelly made sure he was really gone before she came to get me.

"What happened?" She was dying to know.

"He jumped on me and tried to take my shirt off. I can't stay there."

"Oh my God. What are you going to do?" Shelly was a grade below me but she was pretty smart. "Who can you call?"

"I'm going to call Peg, my mom's best friend. I think I can go and stay with her."

Peg had been Mom's best friend for several years. I'm not sure how they met but they had a lot in common. Peg was also a chain-smoking coffee-guzzler, though I liked her a lot. She had two boys, Ricky and Travis, and I enjoyed spending time with them. They were like brothers. Ricky was the younger one and also the naughty one who routinely asked me if I wanted to hump. I always laughed it off and never took him seriously. They were both rambunctious but overall good kids. You could tell Peg really loved her boys and even though she was anxious and neurotic she was a good mom.

My hand was shaking as I dialed the number on the rotary phone.

"Peg? Hi, it's Sparrow." I told her what had happened, how Doug tried to attack me and rip my shirt off and how he was in my bed trying to get me to lie down with him. I tried hard not to cry as I recounted the events to her. I'm still amazed at how I kept my composure.

I was not prepared for the reaction I got.

"Sparrow, stop this nonsense. You're lying. You are just trying to ruin your mother's big moment. How can you do this? I'm not coming to get you. Go back home!" And with that she hung up on me. I was stunned. How could she think I was making this up? It was so embarrassing to begin with. Like I would humiliate myself just to get back at my mom. I needed a plan B.

My best friend in the sixth grade was a girl named Jessica O'Toole. I spent a lot of time at her house and knew her mom really well. Maybe she could help me.

"Hi Jessica, can I talk to your mom?" I was afraid Doug was coming back to look for me so there was no time for small talk.

"Sure," she said as she handed off the phone.

"Mrs. O'Toole, would it be okay if I came and stayed with you for the rest of the week? I'm staying with my step-uncle and I don't feel safe." Thank God this woman picked up on what I was saying right away.

"Is he creepy, honey?"

"Yes," I replied, wiping away the tears of fear and shame I could no longer contain. The O'Tooles had a lot of money and I already felt inferior even though they never said or did anything to make me feel that way. Nevertheless, I was feeling like poor, white trash for real now that I had the proverbial molesting uncle on top of everything else.

I told her where I was and she told me to sit tight until I saw her car pull up in my driveway. She specifically told me she would wait outside until I got there and that she would help me collect my things. I had never felt so protected in all of my life.

She made it over in record time. Shelly and I were by the back door with our faces pressed up against the glass watching for her car. When it pulled up I hugged Shelly and darted over to my house and Mrs. O.

"You let me do all the talking," she said as we approached the back door. She walked right in and Doug was standing there in the kitchen.

"Hi, I'm Stacey. I'm here to help Sparrow collect her things. She's going to be staying with me this week." Doug was speechless and didn't protest.

"Oh...uh, okay," he said as we headed to my room. I packed my things in less than three minutes and we were out of there. We drove in silence for a bit and then Mrs. O. asked me about school. She never brought up the subject of my pervert uncle. She was never a real lovey-dovey, warm woman but she was kind and she saved my ass that day. I admired her firm, direct approach to handling the situation and decided I wanted to be like her. It didn't hurt that she was beautiful, dressed like a million bucks and could paint her nails while driving.

When Mom got home from her wedding/honeymoon she briefly asked me what happened with Doug. I told her everything. She listened, then thought for a moment while using her pinky nail to pick her nose. When mom needed to focus she often picked her nose. She only used her pinky and since her nails were long she didn't have to put it in very far. She would stick it up there then slowly drag her nail down her nostril. It reminded me of digging for gold and grossed me out because Mikey was also a nose picker and would wipe boogers on all the furniture, the carpet, and especially all over the doors in the Rust Puppy. I loathed boogers.

After what seemed like days Mom finally spoke.

"I think we need to keep this incident quiet, Sparrow." I just got married and I don't want anything to jeopardize that, so let's keep this between you and me." I should not have been surprised but I was. I really wanted Mom to stand up for me and protect me like I tried to do for her. I wanted her to scream at Doug and ban him from our house. I wanted her to say "How dare you!" to that pig. But none of that happened, at least not then. I agreed not to discuss it, which let's face it, I wouldn't have done anyway out of pure shame. I felt dirty and disgusting, even though I got away from him. Some old man wanted me and it felt like I had contracted the plague.

With the exception of what happened with Doug my sixth grade year was exactly what I needed to build some confidence and come out of my shell. I was still shy, unsure of myself and felt inferior at times, but I wasn't hiding in bushes and I was able to make friends. I broke up with Conrad because some of the other boys wanted to go out with me but I quickly realized none of them were as kind and sweet as Conrad. I tried to apologize and get him back but he was hurt and not interested. For some reason I thought he'd wait for me as I made the rounds with all of his friends. I wished I could go back and undo the breakup but it was too late. He had already lost that spark for me.

I still finished the sixth grade strong. All As and one B. I was disappointed as I had tried so hard to get straight As. But I was happy, nonetheless. I remember the last day of school. We were all outside playing and my friend Karen and I were making a dance routine to Deniece Williams's "Let's Hear It For the Boy." I felt cool in my Pepto Bismol-pink sweater dress, Mom's black suede boots, and my white lace Madonna glove which I always wore on my left hand because I'm left-handed and proud of it.

Chapter 11

I had no idea what to expect for my seventh grade year but I had heard junior high was really fun. I was a nervous because it was a bigger school and I had gotten comfortable being a big fish in a small pond. Mom and Larry said there was no way they were taking four kids school shopping so they went out one day and picked out all our clothes. I was horrified when Mom came home with lime-green pants for me and shirts with horizontal stripes. These were baby clothes. Couldn't she see I wasn't a baby? I couldn't raid her closet anymore because she was pregnant, getting ready to pop and plus she had been steadily putting on weight since we'd moved in with Larry so there wasn't anything that fit me.

Mom said it was mandatory that I have a seventh-grade physical so she made the appointment with our pediatrician, Dr. Wexler. I didn't think much of it, having been to the doctor on several occasions, mostly for strep. I despised having to say "Ah" and open my mouth while the nurse stuck the tongue depressor that looked like a giant popsicle stick halfway down my throat. I was always afraid I would blow chunks on the nurse. Luckily, I never did.

The morning of the appointment I panicked because I couldn't find any clean underwear. Mom wasn't great at washing clothes and when she did wash them she dried them and dumped them on the folding table in the laundry room. This wouldn't have been the end of the world except we often had ten or more loads of laundry piled high on that table, to the point where it was impossible to find anything. Usually someone had already tried to find a pair of socks so the clothes would be strewn everywhere including on the floor, which often meant they were full of dust, dog hair, and big, black wood spiders. Routinely I was assigned the chore of folding clothes only to lift up a shirt and have a giant, hairy spider jump out, scare me to bits, and go scurrying back into the pile. After several of those occurrences I did my best to avoid folding clothes and since no one else wanted to do it the laundry room morphed into an atomic wasteland.

"Go look downstairs," Mom said when I told her I was out of underwear. I figured that if I scanned the pile long enough I could grab a pair of underwear real quick and avoid a spider. No luck. I moved some clothes around on the floor with my foot. Still no luck.

"Hurry up we have to go!" Mom yelled. I noticed a pair of my brother's underwear sticking out of the pile. Underoos. *Oh God, do I dare?* They weren't bright blue like the Superman ones. Instead, they were light brown. He-man, most likely.

I had never worn my brother's underwear but I had to say they were comfy when I put them on— a little snug, but doable. *I think I can get away with this,* I thought. I threw on the rest of my clothes and off we went.

When we got to the office I had a seat while Mom checked me in. Dr. Wexler came out and ushered me into the office. When I turned around he had closed the door and it was just the two of us.

"Where's my mom?" I asked, feeling uneasy.

"She wanted to wait in the lobby. Now go ahead and get undressed." He stood there staring at me. My heart was pounding and I felt a little lightheaded. *What? Why do I have to get undressed? Where's the tongue depressor?*

"Why do I have to get undressed?"

"So I can give you a proper physical and check you for scoliosis," Dr. Wexler said, irritated.

Feeling exposed, I did as I was told. When I had my white turtleneck with the pastel hearts halfway over my head I remembered a horrifying fact: I was wearing boys' Underoos. Of all the days to wear Mikey's underwear. I stripped down to the Underoos and stood there next to my pile of clothes on the floor. Feeling completely humiliated, I tried to explain.

"I had to wear my brother's underwear today because I ran out of mine." The doctor stood there and stared at me rather wild-eyed. *He must think I'm a total freak.*

"Take your underwear off," he said. Then get on the table."

I froze at first but did as I was told. I got onto the table and lay on my back. Dr. Wexler had an odd look on his face that reminded me of Charles Manson. I had read parts of Mom's paperback copy of *Helter Skelter* which had several pictures of Manson and I recalled those wide, wild eyes. Dr. Wexler looked like he should have had a swastika on his forehead like Mr. Manson.

When he first came to the table he gave me a breast exam, which I thought was bizarre because I had no breasts or breast buds. I had nothing except two little nipples that my brother called blueberries when he could see them through my shirt because I wasn't wearing bras yet. I lay there and let him do his thing, first with one breast, then the other. He was laser focused like he was trying to disarm an explosive and the whole world depended on his expertise. He still had that wild look and I caught a whiff of old man, which was a scent I was familiar with from my days of spending time with Morris.

After a while he moved his way down to my vagina; my pre-pubescent, bare, vagina that had not one single hair on it because I was a little girl. I was eleven, young for starting seventh grade. Even though I was smart and advanced intellectually, I was still just a little girl. Dr. Wexler was highly interested in little girls' bits because he spent quite a few minutes checking the ins and outs of my vagina, spreading my labia and touching what I now know is my clitoris (though back then I still thought it was my mini-penis). He studied it like it was the Hope Diamond or some rare fossil. I felt the blood run out of it—her. Scared, I lay there and intentionally tried to leave my body. It worked a little though I felt my face get hot again as I stared at the ceiling and contemplated how much my life sucked.

"Turn over."

I did as I was told, thinking he was probably done violating my vagina. As soon as I was on my stomach he reached over and spread my butt cheeks apart, using both hands.

"What are you doing?" I asked. I felt too violated to remain silent any longer.

"I'm checking to see if you wipe yourself properly."

For some reason this made me angry. I do *everything* correctly; I know how to wipe my butt. He gave my butt hole the same royal treatment, though I think it was slightly less exciting for him because he didn't spend as much time there and I guess there wasn't as much to see.

When he was satisfied that my butt hole was clean enough Dr. Wexler told me to get off the table and stand touching my toes. He seemed kind of in a rush at this point and spent a whole five seconds on my spine.

"Put your clothes back on," he said.

I dressed quickly, feeling like I could pretend all this had never happened once I had clothes on. I never thought I'd be so happy to put on those Underoos but I was. Thrilled was more like it.

"Mom, why didn't you come in?" I asked when we got to the parking lot.

"Dr. Wexler told me to stay in the waiting room," she said.

"He told me you didn't want to come in. Mom, he made me get naked and he looked up inside me!"

"Oh, really? Maybe that's how they do physicals now. You're getting older and these are things you will have to go through,"

Mom said as she dug around in her disorganized purse looking for a lighter. Six months pregnant and she was still smoking.

"Mom, I'm eleven! He gave me a breast exam and I have no boobs!"

"I think you're overreacting, Sparrow. He's your pediatrician for Chrissake." With that she lit a cigarette and got in the car.

I got in the front passenger seat and held her purse like I often did. Mom's purses were always messy. Instead of cleaning them when they were filled with papers and junk she threw them in her closet and bought a new one. Whenever I needed money for candy I would sneak down into Mom's room and rifle through her bags for change. More than once I found a twenty dollar bill and never told a soul.

Junior high was nothing like I expected. There were so many kids compared with my sixth grade class and they seemed more mature. It didn't take long before I fell back into my old self—quiet, shy and insignificant. I was able to make friends, but I was the wallflower of the clique and too insecure to say much. I felt like all of the girls were better, prettier, and more confident than I was. The boys I had gone to school with the year before were now interested in the new girls and couldn't care less about me. I was that like that pack of stale saltine crackers at the bottom of Mom's purse that you eat only when you are desperately hungry or sick from the flu. I was irrelevant.

The school work in junior high was more rigorous. I wasn't crazy about any of my teachers but one stands out as possibly the unhappiest person I had ever met—my homeroom teacher, Lila Carpenter. I never saw that woman smile once the entire time I was in her class. She had dark brown hair styled in a pixie cut and pointy ears that made her look like an elf, albeit a mean one. She hated all children but she had a special loathing for my classmate, Dexter Whitefield. He was in my homeroom class and had some sort of ADD mixed with an impish spirit. That kid lived to torture Mrs. Carpenter, which actually made homeroom somewhat bearable. The only days Dexter didn't get sent to the principal's office were the days he was absent. He loved to make Mrs. Carpenter's face turn red with fury and every day he came up with a clever new way to do so. The class laughed hysterically at his antics.

Even though Dexter reminded me of my brother, I liked him because it was fun to see someone else get tortured for a change. He was never mean to me like some other boys who called me "Notacious Tatas" because of my flat chest. One of those boys was Justin Shaw, the boy who had called me gorilla arms all through the fifth grade. He had moved away only to come back in seventh grade and sit right in front of me in homeroom. I'll bet he didn't even remember me and the whole gorilla arms shtick. Now he and Brad Wilson cracked each other up making fun of my flat chest. I had not yet discovered padded bras.

Chapter 12

Mom gave birth to Doodie that December. She finally got to name a daughter Christy Ann and she was delighted; however, we never once called her that. We had given her the nickname Scootie when she started scooting across the floor but she wasn't able to say it. She would refer to herself as Doodie and one day it stuck. She was our Doodie.

Doodie was a planned baby. Mom and Larry had sat us kids down one night after dinner and told us they were pregnant. We knew they were trying and we were horrified at the thought of another person in the house. Katie threw herself down half a flight of stairs when she found out, wailing of course. I say half a flight because we lived in a tri-level so it was only about six steps to the landing, but I'm sure it hurt. I was disgusted at the thought of Mom and Larry doing it, and also because there would be one more person sharing the bathroom. "Another baby will bond our family," Mom said. I didn't believe her.

Mom was fairly happy throughout the pregnancy. I'm not sure why because I had heard pregnancy was the pits, but Mom handled it well. She didn't give up smoking, but she insisted she had cut down. I didn't believe her, though she may have been telling the truth because she put on a lot of weight. Doodie ended up being a ten pound baby which may not sound like a lot but coming out of a woman under five feet tall it's quite a feat. So much so that Mom had to have her first C-section after giving birth naturally three previous times.

I had a cold on December eighth, the day Mom delivered Doodie, so I had to wear a mask to go see them. As soon as I saw her lots of ice instantly melted off my heart. I couldn't hold her that day but I still fell in love in a heartbeat. Luckily the other kids felt the same. We all had a new focus—the baby.

Mom was right about a baby bonding the family. The fighting decreased for a while and everyone had a spring in their step. Doodie never cried much which made her all the more loveable. I couldn't wait to get home after school so I could play with her, dress her up and just be in her presence. Mom was thankful she had so much help and didn't need to cut down on her cigarette or coffee time at all. She didn't even seem to mind that Doodie called me "Mom" more than once. Part of me loved it and part of me felt guilty, worrying that Mom's feelings would be hurt. Whenever she said it I always corrected her.

Doodie started crawling at a very young age. By seven months she was moving around the house pretty well. It was hard to catch her once she got going but she never got into much mischief. Well, until I taught her how.

One afternoon I was changing her diaper on the floor in the living room. Out of the corner of my eye I happened to notice Larry's wallet on the edge of the breakfast bar. No one was around so I ran over to grab it while Doodie was still lying on the floor. I hadn't seen Larry change many diapers and I wondered why. It irritated me, not that I minded helping Doodie, but why was I changing so many of these things? Her number twos were stinky, probably from all the breast milk. I gave the wallet to Doodie to occupy her while I was putting a new diaper on her. This time it was just a number one so I was relieved.

Doodie had pulled out Larry's driver's license and was trying to eat it. Once her new diaper was on I conveniently showed her she could stuff things in it, like her daddy's license. She was fascinated, and I could tell she wondered why she hadn't realized sooner that her diaper was a pocket, of sorts. She proceeded to empty the contents of the wallet and stick everything in her diaper: a five dollar bill, some business cards, and a few phone numbers on torn pieces of paper. When she was finished she dumped the wallet and scooted away. I was excited about her next diaper change and would make sure it wasn't from me.

As luck would have it later that afternoon little Doodie laid a huge brick in her Huggies. What was even better was that Larry had the honor of changing it. *God does hear prayers,* I thought as I heard the commotion in the family room. Now the hardest part was going to be acting innocent and surprised at the news of a seven-month-old expert thief among us.

"Do you know anything about this?" Larry asked, as he held up his poop-smeared driver's license.

"What happened?" I really wasn't much of a liar but I was a prankster and that somehow made fibbing okay

"Doodie emptied out my wallet and put everything in her diaper. I'm sure she didn't do that on her own."

"Oh come on. No one would give your wallet to Doodie. Plus, she's pretty smart. I guess she figured out she has a place to put things."

"Well, she *is* a smart cookie," Larry agreed. No one could ever get mad at Doodie. She was easygoing and smiled all the time. She smelled like baby which was even better than the puppy smell. She also loved to cuddle. She was a living, breathing, baby doll.

It didn't take long for the other kids to come out and roll on the floor when they saw Doodie had pooped on a five dollar bill. No one outwardly suspected me since I was Oscar-worthy for keeping a straight face. Later that night I couldn't take it and I told Punky.

"Hey, you know the whole wallet thing?" I whispered. "It was me."

"I kinda figured," she said. We had a nice sister giggle. The great thing was I could always trust Punky to have my back. She never once ratted me out and it was soothing to have that one person you could trust, even if she was only seven.

Mom always had a lot of anxiety but after Doodie was born she experienced post-partum depression. She was tired all the time and struggled to get out of bed. She was snapping at Larry and us kids for everything. She was zoning out more and more, and smoking up a storm. Mom's obstetrician, Dr. Harlan, referred Mom to her husband, a psychologist named Donald, to help her deal with her anxiety and depression. Donald started seeing Mom once a week for therapy and also sent her to his office partner, Dr. Robertson, a psychiatrist, who prescribed Mom a nice cocktail of Ativan and Klonopin. I know because once she started taking them she said their names on a daily basis. "I need an Ativan," or "Shit, I'm out of Klonopin." These medications became staples in our house much like the Pepsi and Entenmann's Mom still bought weekly.

Mom had a crush on Donald. She talked about him nonstop and when she did she had a wistful look in her eye, like a schoolgirl in love. I saw that look on my friends all the time so I knew it well. I knew Donald because more than once I wound up sitting in the waiting room while Mom had her session. Once Mom forced me to have a session with him because she thought I was becoming mouthy and defiant. They spent the entire fifty minutes taking turns yelling at me and telling me I was going down the wrong path. He was irritated with me, but then again I think he had a thing for Mom too. She was still beautiful even though she had put on weight and Mom could make any man fall for her. Who knows what they were really doing on that couch?

Mom's behavior seemed to get worse after she began treatment. I don't know if it was a combination of bad therapy mixed with the drugs but throughout my teen years I watched her steadily decline. Mom talked about her past in therapy because she always brought it up in times of stress.

"Donald says I wasn't ever loved as a child, which is why I need these pills now," she told me. "Smoking helps reduce anxiety," was another one of her favorites. Why didn't Donald ever tell her to take a walk? Go to an ashram? Read a fucking self-help book? Mom did have her art and she was damned good too, until the pills zoned her out too much and she couldn't finish a painting. Her skill also declined and paintings started to look more Dali-esque over time, with strange characters painted randomly in the corner of the picture. I was pissed because it was one of her only skills and I was actually proud to show my friends her work, even though she painted lots of nudes which I thought were inappropriate for a mother to be doing.

* * *

"Sparrow, I have a question," Mikey said as I entered his room. He was still in his bed (having just awakened) and had called me in as I was headed to the bathroom. Mikey went back and forth between living at Dad's and living with us. He could never make up his mind about where he wanted to be and both parents bribed him with toys, electronics, and the like. This month he was living with us.

I was curious about his question because Mikey never spoke to me unless it was to say something mean or derogatory. At twelve, he was finally evolving out of his all-out meltdowns (thank God) but had replaced this behavior with nonstop teasing and harassing. Anyone in his line of sight was a target. Even the poor dogs.

Mikey teased me about my "big, fat pooper" at least once a day.

"God, Sparrow, look at that big fat pooper! It's so huge! No one's ever gonna ask you out with that thing. How do you get through life with such a fat pooper?" He went on and on and cracked himself up until I finally backhanded him or chased him out of the room. Mikey also teased me about my flat chest, how I got a C in a class once, and how I inherited Dad's crooked toes. More than once he referred to me as "Lumpy Toes" and he would grab at them if I wasn't wearing socks.

"What is it?" I sat at the foot of his bed.

"How come when I wake up in the morning my underwear is sticky?" he asked, careful to avoid making eye contact. I was briefly stunned by this question, but it didn't take me long to think on my feet and I immediately saw an opportunity for some comeuppance regarding the relentless teasing I experienced on a daily basis.

"Oh..." I said, looking down, trying to be dramatic.

How fun, my brother is having nocturnal emissions.

"What? What is it?"

How fun is this going to be.

"Well, it means you're getting your period," I said, completely straight-faced.

"That's not true! Only girls get periods!"

"Well, actually that's not true. Boys get them too only they are too embarrassed to talk about them."

"Really? Oh."

"This is exciting!" I continued. "This means you're becoming a man." With that he perked up a bit.

"So what do I do?" he asked. His eyes were big and he reminded me of a baby bird. For a second he looked so innocent and sweet. I almost told him I was kidding, but then I remembered my big fat pooper, and how he teased me about *my* period.

"Well, you should go get some of Mom's pads and start wearing them to school in case you get it. You don't want to have a mess in your pants and bleed on the carpet like I did, do you?"

"No!" he cried and with that he had jumped out of bed and dashed into the bathroom. I guess he figured it out because I didn't have to explain how to use them. Mom, incidentally, used the largest maxi pads on the market. Today they are called Depends but back then they were just gigantic, industrial-strength pads the size of your forearm. I had resorted to using one when I had run out of my own pads and I remember it being so large that when I sat down it felt like I was sitting on a cloud only it wasn't at all comfortable and it went right up my butt. But Mikey didn't know the difference.

Every day I checked in with Mikey when he got home from school.

"So, did you get it?"

"Not yet, Sparrow," he replied, excited about the thought of getting a period. I wondered if it had something to do with being in love with that pink bike years ago but I didn't dwell. I was having way too much fun.

A week later Mom was in the bathroom one afternoon and called out, "Who is using all of my pads?" Before I could speak Mikey piped up.

"Me, Mom. I'm getting my period and I want to be prepared."

"Sparrow!" Mom was none too pleased upon hearing about Mikey's journey into womanhood. How did she know this would involve me? "How long have you been wearing pads?" Mom asked Mikey.

"All week, Mom. It could come at any moment."

I was in my room on my bed in a hysterical fit of laughter. I laughed so hard I hyperventilated. I cried giant, happy tears of vengeance and nothing was going to take them away.

"You're grounded!" Mom stormed into my room which was right across the bathroom so she only had to stomp her feet three times.

"That's okay, it's so worth it," I replied when I could speak.

"Your brother's going to be screwed up and it will be your fault!" Even that guilt trip couldn't quell my laughter. If Mom couldn't tell how screwed up Mikey was by now then she was crazier than I thought. There was no way I was taking the blame for that mess.

Mom decided she should address my brother's wet dreams and his entrance into puberty by asking Larry to "give him the talk." Later she regretted it.

After dinner one night Mom asked Larry if he had talked to Mikey.

"Yeah, I handled it," he replied as if he were saying "Yes, I took out the trash."

"Well, what did you say?"

"Not much. I took him into the bathroom and showed him how to put on a condom."

"What? Why on Earth would you do that?"

"Don't you want him to practice safe sex?" It was obvious he thought he had done the good deed of the century.

"He's only twelve, Larry, I don't think he was ready for all of that. Did you give him any advice at least?"

"Sure. I told him not to use the condom on Damon," Larry replied, laughing like crazy. Damon was Mikey's best friend who lived across the street. They hung out all the time and were always getting into some kind of mischief together.

"Dear God." Mom sighed, rolled her eyes and lit a cigarette. Even I felt bad for Mikey at that point. His only birds and bees talk was *Don't be gay*. It looked like I was going to have to handle that one too.

That spring Mom decided to take us to Disney World for spring break. Doodie was three now and Mom thought she was old enough to enjoy meeting the princesses. Larry was gearing up for his spring season but he decided he would come on the trip with all of us first. I was less than thrilled.

As luck would have it Mikey had fractured his ankle doing jumps with Damon on their bikes a month before. By this time Mikey had upgraded from the pink Huffy to an actual boy's BMX bike, however I think having the tough bike made him take extra risks and he ended up with some pretty good injuries.

I was excited to spend some time in Florida because Mom said we were going to Daytona Beach where you could actually drive your car on the sand near the water. I was also looking forward to seeing Doodie's reaction to all the Disney characters and I wanted to take her on some rides. She had stopped calling me Mom by this point but we were still close and I thought she was the most precious thing on the planet.

Mikey got his cast off a day or two before we left. He wasn't able to put much pressure on his leg so Mom got him crutches to take on the trip. I just knew it wasn't going to go well, with his total lack of resiliency combined with his frequent whining. I decided I would keep my Walkman with me at all times and do my best to ignore him.

I was right about Mikey whining. His foot hurt a lot and he was letting everyone know. It made him more whiny in general—it was too hot, or too cold, or he didn't like his food, and on and on. The sucky thing about going on vacation with your family is that you are trapped with them. Larry was trying his best not to react, but I could see the steam seeping out of his ears. I had sneaked a few cigarettes in my suitcase for the trip and thought I probably didn't pack enough. I wondered how Larry had never taken up smoking, but then I remembered he had his own vice and her name was Little Debbie.

Things were tense but manageable the night we got in. I was disappointed at the choice of our run-down hotel, where everything was decorated in brown and industrial orange. It had a pool and that was all I really cared about, but I did search the bed for bugs every night before I got in, which I always did after getting bit by a spider a few years back. The doctor said the spider had probably crawled into my bed because I was bit on the back of the leg and I didn't recall it happening. This wasn't any ordinary spider bite either. It was the size of a silver dollar and I had to keep a bandage on it because it oozed pus. Mom had to take me to the local doctor several times to have it cleaned and bandaged, which was painful and disgusting but at least she wasn't dragging me back to Dr. Wexler so I felt relatively safe. She had said to be thankful that the skin wasn't turning black because people sometimes lose body parts from spider bites. Her comment triggered an instant full-on spider phobia. I'm sure she didn't mean for that to happen; she was just making conversation.

I was truly looking forward to the next day since we were going to Magic Kingdom. I forgot how long it took Mom to get ready for anything, especially because even on vacation she wanted to sit for hours and make love to her coffee and cigarettes. Larry was irritated but still holding it together. He was more laid back when he was out of his environment, and he had not made a single comment about us not being his kids and having to pay for things. Perhaps he was seeing Dr. Robertson now as well and had gotten on some new state-of-the-art, heavy duty, mind-altering, solve all your problems antidepressant. I was beginning to enjoy seeing his face stay the same shade of normal-person flesh.

I should have known something was up because things were going so smoothly. Soon after we got to the park Mom dropped the bomb. "Your brother is going to have to be in a wheelchair all day because of his ankle and you need to push him."

No wonder the mutants were being so nice to me! And by nice I mean they weren't yelling or screaming or threatening to cut me open and sell my kidney on the black market to pay for all the electricity I used when I forgot to turn off my bedroom light. *Fuck. Fuck shit!* I was a high schooler now and I was sure there was some clause in the instruction manual that said I was exempt from pushing my loser of a brother in a wheelchair at Magic Kingdom.

"I'm not pushing him! He's *your* son. You push him!"

"I'm pushing your sister and Larry's in charge of pictures. You have to push him. You kids can take turns but you're in charge."

Larry had brought his big, fancy Olympus 35mm camera because he thought he missed his real calling as a photographer. He was always bragging about how good he was at taking pictures but I didn't think anything he shot was that great, though he could have won a Pulitzer and I still would have thought it was shit.

Mom knew I'd never suggest sweet little Punky push our brother around for any length of time, though Punky would have if I asked her to. She was only nine and he was kind of a chunk and I wanted her to enjoy the park. I didn't mind if Katie pushed but Mikey teased her and made her cry and I didn't see her being able to tolerate it for long. There was no way out of this for me.

I put my sunglasses on and took solace in the fact that no one would recognize me. Of course no boys would be checking me out pushing a wheelchair but that was my own fault. How did I not see this coming? How could I let myself believe this would actually be a vacation for me too? I decided to suck it up and just push the little turd biscuit.

Things were fine at first, and when I say fine I really mean soul-crushing but that wasn't a foreign experience for me so I was able to deal relatively well. I pushed Mikey to each ride and sometimes he got on sooner because of the whole wheelchair bit. I tried to spend some time with my sisters but he'd start in on his whine routine so that was impossible.

"I wanna go this way!" he cried when he didn't get his way. Sometimes I stopped so I could take a picture with my own camera and he would start his whining again. "Mom, she's not pushing me!"

"Push your brother, Sparrow," she said between drags of her cigarette. Mom smoked her way through Disney, saying that crowds made her anxious and smoking was the only thing that calmed her. I thought maybe there was some rule against smoking in the park but she couldn't care less and no one said anything to her.

When we got to Cinderella's castle I could barely contain my excitement. I never got that Disney trip with Grandpa Johnny so it was great fun to relive those lost moments with Doodie. She and I had watched the movie over and over and I was really hoping she'd get to meet Cinderella in the flesh. I had to push Mikey all through the castle and if I left the wheelchair for an instant he was yelling for Mom. I was missing out and the rage bubbled up from the soles of my feet. I tried to quell it, knowing that if it reached my chest I was in big trouble. Mom got to smoke her calm sticks, but I had none. I tried my best to remain human.

Cinderella was nowhere to be found. It must have been her lunch hour, or perhaps she was taking a smoke break. I couldn't imagine having to work around kids all day in the sweltering heat in that heavy dress. I had seen pictures of her in the pamphlet and had instantly thought I would never want her job.

When we came out the other side of the castle the path was downhill. I realized I needed to be safe so I tried to slow my pushing so I didn't lose control of Mikey's wheelchair. "Push faster!" he demanded in that whiny voice that made me want to crawl under a rock but not before completely knocking his block off. I'm not sure what happened next, but the rage swelled like a tidal wave and I couldn't contain the power or force of it.

"Okay, you want fast?" I asked as I gave the chair a giant push and sent him careening down the hill for the best ride so far that day. Well, at least for me.

Mikey wailed like he was being attacked by zombies. He did his best to slow his speed by trying to grab the wheels but he wasn't successful and I could tell the wheels were hurting his dainty little hands. People stopped what they were doing and stared. Mom left the stroller and made a weak attempt at running after Mikey, all the while screaming, "My son! My son!" like a good Italian madre. I stood there, completely shocked at what I had done. My reason and wit then returned and I decided I needed to make it look like an accident, though I failed miserably because shock turned into an uncontrollable fit of laughter.

I was lucky that Mikey didn't crash hard or injure more body parts. He was able to slow himself down enough to plow into a trash can. The only thing hurt was his little ego.

"Sparrow!" Mom screamed from the bottom of the hill. "Come down here!"

I made my way down and there was a crowd gawking and sticking around, waiting to see my fate.

"Mom, it was a total accident."

"He could have really hurt himself! You're grounded! Larry, take her back to the hotel."

I could tell Larry was torn. On one hand, he hated me and typically jumped on any excuse to ground me. On the other, he hated Mikey more, and I had seen the glimmer in his eye as Mikey's wheelchair was careening down the hill. He must have had to bite back hard on his own laughter.

"Come on, Sparrow," he said as he motioned me to the path that led to the gate. "You gotta go back."

Neither parent realized that sending me back to the hotel to sit at the pool and smoke Newport Lights was the best thing that happened to me that day. I spent the afternoon in total peace reading *Cosmo* and praying the freak show family stayed away as long as possible.

* * *

My first sexual experience in high school was at a party at Jessica's house in freshman year. We were all drinking and I made out with Brian McMurty, a kid I had met in sixth grade. We were in Jessica's room, lying on the bed. He was on top of me but we still had our clothes on. The room was dark and one minute we were kissing and the next he had somehow undone his pants and jammed his penis in my face.

"Come on, put it in your mouth," he begged.

I was a little drunk and the room was spinning. I had a quick flashback to my former crush, Bryan Sweeney. He sat in front of me in algebra and I loved him instantly. He was the cutest guy I had ever seen and he wore the best-smelling cologne, which I later found out was Brut by Fabergé. He used to pick me up at night when I sneaked out and we drove around for hours making out in the back of his friend Mark's Jeep. Bryan always tried to put his hand up my shirt and I always swatted it away. He broke up with me to go out with Janey Smith because it was rumored she gave great hand jobs.

I was feeling a twinge of guilt mixed with bewilderment. Why would I put *this* Brian's penis in my mouth when he wasn't my boyfriend and I wouldn't even let the boy I wanted to marry touch my blueberries? Before I could answer he was poking my face with his very hard dick which was alarming because he couldn't see what he was doing and I was afraid he'd put one of my eyes out. I reached up, opened wide and guided it through my lips and making sure that my teeth didn't get in the way. I didn't have to do much work because he was doing the in and out part. I just needed to make sure I didn't throw up. I'm pretty sure this was his first blow job because (thank you, Jesus) it didn't last long. His stickiness went everywhere but I didn't care because I'd much rather have it in my hair than down my throat. I'd heard that experienced girls swallowed but I was new at this and didn't want to take my chances, especially after an evening of Southern Comfort and wine coolers.

When it was over we lay there for a minute, then he said he was going back to the party. He pulled his pants up and left, leaving the light off, which was the nicest part of that evening as I didn't have to look at myself in the full-length mirrored closet doors right in front of Jessica's bed.

After freshman year I went to stay with Dad for the summer, like always. This particular year he was living in Birmingham, Alabama in an upscale townhouse complex. He had gotten a new sales job there though I never heard about what happened with his last job. Dad changed jobs a lot and I wasn't sure why though I figured it had something to do with his being opinionated and assertive when it came to speaking his mind. Dad didn't have much respect for authority, which probably didn't go over well in the workplace.

I was bored as usual, cooped up in the apartment with Mikey. I didn't have friends but there was a pool so I spent most days there reading and working on my tan. Sometimes I made myself a drink with Dad's liquor and sipped on it all afternoon. Sometimes I chose the vodka, other times the rum and every once in a while I got into the whiskey. I tried to vary it up so it wasn't obvious that I was drinking all of his booze, though Dad didn't much mind if I drank. A few years back when he had a sailboat he let me have wine coolers here and there on the water and it was no big deal. I developed a liking for having a drink or two while sunbathing and reading. I never got drunk, but it was nice to have a buzz that took the edge off and eased the loneliness. I still hated leaving my friends each summer knowing they were all having fun without me. The year before several of them wrote me letters and cards but this year there were none.

Dad was pretty busy with his new job but occasionally he would come home after work and teach Mikey and me how to play tennis. I wasn't at all coordinated but I loved it nonetheless. I had no idea Dad even knew how to play, but I was always learning things like that about him. Mikey picked up the game much faster than I did, so he and Dad played more often, though somehow it would turn into a yelling match and giant competition. I didn't want to be a part of that drama so I quit going to the courts with them.

One evening about halfway through my summer vacation I was walking back from the pool when a car pulled up and asked me for directions. Not just any car, but a shiny new black Ford Mustang GT.

"Excuse me, do you know where apartment 312 is?" asked the driver. I didn't know exactly but I had a vague idea and I tried to point him in the right direction. "How about you hop in and show me where you think it is." He reached over and opened the passenger-side door.

I quickly assessed the situation. The driver was delivering pizzas and was probably only a few years older than me. He looked like a young Tom Cruise with lighter hair, and eyes so blue he could have been part husky. I hopped in the car and my heart beat a little faster. I liked taking risks and this one seemed fairly safe. After a very boring month I needed some excitement and I was hoping this was it.

We drove around the complex until we found 312. During that time Mustang told me he had just graduated high school and was off to college in the fall. The car was his graduation present. I couldn't believe I was sitting in a beautiful car with a Tom Cruise look-alike college boy. I told him the truth—that I had just finished my freshman year, that I was only fourteen, and that I was bored to tears living in that apartment complex with no friends.

"You're only fourteen? Wow, I have a brother your age," he said, looking confused. I was convinced I came across a bit more mature than his little brother, with my large sunglasses, my mostly empty mug of Jack and Coke and the latest copy of *Vogue* in hand.

"Can I get your number?" Mustang asked, grinning as we pulled up close to where I lived.

"Sure." I jotted it down for him on a pizza box. "Nice meeting you," I said as I walked away, feeling his eyes on me. I decided not to turn around as I let myself in the front door.

It didn't take Mustang long to call and make plans.

"Hey, I'm off at eight, how about we meet at the pool?"

I said yes not knowing exactly how I'd pull it off. Dad wasn't keen on letting me date. I didn't even bother asking because if he found out I was talking with a college boy he'd come unglued and I wasn't risking it. I figured I could make something up to at least get out for a little while. It wouldn't be that hard, especially since Dad was usually asleep in his chair by eight anyway.

Luckily Dad was asleep, remote in hand, when I decided to go out for an "evening swim." I was sure to tell Samantha who said it was fine and my heart raced as I walked down to the pool. When I got there Mustang was hanging out in the hot tub. "Come on in," he said as I put my stuff down on a nearby table. I stepped in and sat across from him so I could look him in the eye and read his intentions. We were the only two people in the pool area which relaxed me a bit. We talked about school, friends and college. He asked me what New England was like because he had never been that far north. It didn't take long, however, for him to inch over close to me and start a full-on make out fest. And to tell the truth, I was hoping for it. I had deemed him "safe" and decided he would be the perfect summer fling, though I had not yet decided how far I wanted to be flung.

Mustang and I met up a few nights a week either by the pool or in the clubhouse and we spent most of our time in complete make-out mode. He was aggressive which I liked, but it also made me not fall for him. He wasn't sweet enough to be any sort of boyfriend material but I did like the primitive nature of his groping and feeling me up. I had only kissed a few boys and I had never experienced anything like that. It was intense. Urgent. I kept meeting up with him because it was much better than sitting inside watching TV or writing in my dear diary about how bored I was. At least with Mustang I was experiencing life and learning about the birds and the bees at the same time.

Mustang was the first boy I let touch my vagina. There was a certain safety in knowing I'd be going back home soon and no one would ever know about it. I figured he could break it in somehow, kind of like a new glove. He delighted in the fact that no one had ever touched it before, which was mostly true. I certainly wasn't going to tell him about Dr. Wexler, which was completely different on every level.

I knew next to nothing about my vagina and Mustang was happy to educate me. I had never even used a tampon so I was nervous. I had gotten my period the summer before, when Dad and Samantha were living in Dallas. They happened to be out of town that weekend, at a party in New England that Dad's sister Catherine was throwing, something related to work. They left Mikey and me alone with our older stepsister, Carla. She was fifteen and in her own world, and wanted little to do with us. She had no desire to sit down and discuss periods with me, or anything else for that matter. I didn't find out until much later that she was pregnant that summer. Perhaps no one had discussed periods with her, either.

The morning I got it I woke up with the worst stomach cramps ever. I was nauseous and dizzy and it felt like someone had kicked me in between my legs. I crawled out of bed and headed down the hall to the bathroom. As soon as I sat down I realized what had happened. My underwear was blood-soaked and more blood was pouring into the toilet like a faucet that's ninety-percent turned off but still running. I had learned about periods in school but I wasn't paying close attention, perhaps because the thought of blood coming out of me anywhere was a real turn-off. I had gotten several bloody noses in my life and thought they were the worst thing on the planet, so I was emotionally unprepared for this rite of passage.

"Carla, I just got my period, what do I do?" I asked, as she was eating her breakfast and watching TV.

"I don't know, is there anything in the bathroom?"

"No, there's nothing." Samantha had gotten a hysterectomy several years before and had no need for feminine products and, as I later found out, neither did Carla.

"Tell Mikey to go to the store," she suggested. I knew that was a long shot but I decided to bribe him. Just as I was about to go find him he came walking into the living room, curious.

"Who bled on the carpet? Is the dog injured?"

Great. I bled on Samantha's white carpet.

"Hey, I got my period and I need you to go to the store for me. I need pads," I said as sweetly as I could, which was hard seeing as I was in some intense pain.

"You got your period on the carpet? That's disgusting!" Mikey replied as he started in with his relentless teasing. "Sparrow got her period. I can't wait until Dad sees that you ruined his carpet." And on and on he went. I just let him do his thing, hoping if he got it all out he would be more inclined to go to the 7-Eleven.

"Dude, I have five bucks for you if you go get me pads. Think of how much candy that will buy." Surprisingly he agreed, and I felt a surge of relief. No one had thought to give me a period starter kit but if Mikey could come through for me I was golden.

It took him forever to go down to the store and back, even though he rode his bike. When he returned he had a huge bag of candy and threw a box of Tampax at me.

"I can't use these, they're tampons," I said, exasperated. "You need to go back."

"I'm not going back! The guy behind the counter asked if they were for me," he said, embarrassed.

"Mikey, please!" I was getting desperate. I would have gone myself but I was bleeding like crazy and I didn't trust the wad of toilet paper I had stuck in my underwear to hold me to the store and back. And I was in so much pain from the cramps I could barely stand up straight. I asked Carla who laughed like I was nuts to even think she would go out of her way for me. I had no choice but to harass Mikey until he relented.

He was back within five minutes this time and threw a paper bag at me. Inside were several industrial-strength pads which was a relief, but they weren't in a box.

"Where did you get these?" I asked.

"From Brett. He said his sister just got her period too and he put the pads in a bag for you. He said to tell you congratulations."

"You went to Brett's?" Brett was the slightly older boy who lived next door and I had a total crush on him. "I'm going to kill you!"

I forgot all about my cramps and chased Mikey around the house. He ran into his room and held the door shut as I tried to push my way in. I gave up out of necessity and went to retrieve the paper bag. *My first pad*, I thought, as I stuck it into a fresh pair of underwear. It was uncomfortable and scraped the sides of my legs when I walked, well, waddled. I was convinced people would be able to tell I was wearing a small pillow between my legs. I would need to figure out this tampon stuff eventually, but in that moment I was content doing what girls on their period did—read magazines, watch TV and eat a pint of Ben and Jerry's. Later I found out both Ben *and* Jerry happened to be at the party my parents went to in Vermont.

I thought about sharing with Mustang that nothing had ever been stuck up in there but I was too embarrassed. I just went with it. Mustang showed me how my vagina would get wet when we made out and that it made it easier for him to stick his finger inside me. I really liked the way it felt and for some reason was embarrassed because I liked it. One time he tried to stick two fingers inside me and I let out a yelp.

"Wow, girl, you're so tight I can only use one finger. We should keep you that way." I later realized that was his subtle way of saying he wasn't going to take my virginity. I don't think I would have gone there anyway, but I'm glad I didn't face that temptation. Mustang was happy to keep it innocent. Maybe he had a sweet side after all? Or maybe he knew a bit about statutory rape.

The night before I left to go back to New England Mustang stopped over to say goodbye. We were sitting outside on the curb in front of Dad's place, talking and holding hands.

"I'm so glad I met you this summer," he said with a goofy grin. I was really glad too. Our clandestine meetings had added some much-needed spice to my life. I leaned over and gave him a hug.

"What the hell are you doing out here?" I heard someone bellow from behind me. Dad had woken up from his Barcalounger slumber and realized I was outside. There he was, standing in his blue, velvet monogrammed skirt, sans shirt, looking about eight months pregnant. Dad's evening attire alternated between his Hugh Hefner smoking robe and his mail-order catalog monogrammed velvet wrap that Velcroed on one side. Of course he would be wearing the skirt. I didn't even know they made skirts for men other than kilts until I saw Dad wearing one.

"Dad, I'll be right in. Give me five minutes."

Dad grumbled something as he turned around and went back in the house. I was grateful he didn't try to introduce himself to Mustang since he was half-awake and reeked of Coors Light, *and* was wearing a skirt.

"I guess this is goodbye," Mustang said as we stood up. He gave me one last hug and a lingering kiss. I stood on the curb and waved as he drove away. I wasn't the least bit sad that I would never see him again. Instead I was elated that I'd had an adventurous summer after all.

That same year Mikey decided to live with Dad again. I thought it was a fabulous idea not only because there would be one less person using our only bathroom but also because Larry was growing more and more pissed at my brother. He couldn't stand to even be in the same room and the arguing and fighting were getting worse by the day. I could see how Mikey could be unnerving, but Larry had no patience and took out all of his frustrations on him. Larry only worked six months out of the year, which meant he was mostly home for the other six, unless he was plowing snow, so there was little reprieve. He was constantly looking for chores for us to do and Mikey was having none of it. So he went back to Dad's.

At first, it was quiet. And almost livable. I picked up more of the slack and that sucked, but I could handle it if there was peace. No one calling me fat, no one constantly making fart noises or wiping boogers on every piece of furniture in the house. Mom was bereft that her only son was gone and she cried for him a lot, but Mom cried about stuff all the time anyway so really what did it matter?

The reprieve was short-lived. I had overlooked one simple fact. Since Mikey was the one Larry took almost all of his frustrations out on and I was the oldest, second mouthiest kid, his ire would trickle down to me. Larry hyper-focused on me more and more and took an unhealthy interest in what I was doing. High school had introduced me to boys, booze and occasional bong hits. All of these things were readily available at my school so I was having the time of my life.

I was away from home more and more and the endless list of chores wasn't getting done on time. Larry wanted to put an abrupt stop to all of that, so I was grounded. A lot. I had taken a liking to talking back because it was my only defense mechanism. I became highly adept at arguing and learned how to cut deep with my words. That was a skill I only practiced with Mom a nd Larry but I felt like they totally deserved it.

"Sparrow, you're grounded!" Larry said once for God-knows-what.

"Whatever, go fuck yourself."

"Now you're grounded for a month!"

"Great. Go fuck yourself."

"Make that three months!"

"Awesome. Go fuck yourself."

"Six months!"

"You can still go fuck yourself,"

That was a fairly common occurrence. He would go on to ground me for twelve years and then realize how ridiculous he sounded which meant that I'd won. I became good at winning. I realized how ignorant and ridiculous my parents were and lost respect for them when I realized I was way more intelligent than both of them put together.

Chapter 13

As I got older and became more jaded the fighting intensified. My relationship with Mom was suffering because her anger and depression were growing worse day by day. After she lost a custody battle for Mikey she grew to resent me. It's a long story and not really mine to tell but shortly after Mikey went to live with Dad he started complaining to Mom about how bad it was, so she did what any good Mom would do— she kidnapped her son back. One day she decided to fly to the Midwest where Dad was living, pick my brother up from school and bring him back home. The worst part was that Mikey really didn't want to come back; he was just complaining to get attention. My parents went back to court and fought over my pawn of a brother.

Right off the bat Mom had insisted I testify against my father so she could keep her son. She wanted me to tell the judge about Dad's drinking and drug use. I refused. There was no way I was getting in the middle of any more of their arguing. They hadn't been on good terms for years and they were always bashing each other, though Mom was worse about it.

The day Mom came home from court after losing the custody battle she went for me, and when I say she went for me I mean she lunged at me full force and tried to strangle the life out of me.

"You!" she screamed as she came charging toward me, arms outstretched. She attempted to grab my throat with both hands, screaming about how she'd lost her son and it was all my fault. Peg was there that day along with Larry and it took both of them to get Mom off me. Even though they stopped Mom from killing me they both blamed me too. I could tell from their looks and their body language that they thought I should have gone to court and testified against Dad. I knew in my soul staying out of it was the right thing. I could have had the ultimate revenge on Dad for stealing me all those years ago and nearly ruining my life, but I didn't hate my father, and I thought Mikey was better off away from Larry.

Mom was also envious of my high school years and that I had friends and boyfriends and a life. Mom was trapped in her home with her controlling husband and whiny children, her looks fading by the minute. I was coming out of my shell, going to parties and enjoying life. She was jealous.

"You're not going anywhere!" Mom screamed one night as I was leaving. "You're outta control!"

Sure I was living it up, but I was nowhere near out of control and I knew it. I saw many of my friends barfing in the bathroom at school after lunch, shagging every boy that came along and drinking beer in between classes. She didn't know what she was talking about.

"Why would I take any advice from you, you three-time loser?" I wholly expected her to yell back some horrendous obscenity but she didn't. The look on her face contorted into sheer anguish, and she let out a wail like someone had just said the meanest thing on the planet to her, and then I realized that I just had. I stood there speechless as she turned, covered her face in shame and ran away. Technically I had won that round, but it didn't feel like any kind of victory. Seeing Mom's pained face pierced my heart and I realized I'd gone too far.

We had never discussed the fact that she had children with three different men but I guess it weighed on her to some degree. I hadn't planned that comment; it just came out. On some level I was ashamed of her. What woman marries three losers? I was disappointed in her taste in men, especially since her choices affected me. I was sick of these assholes ruining my life in some way and I was rebelling.

We never spoke of that fight and what I had said after that day, though she kept her distance for a while. I was okay with that even though I had some nagging guilt. I had officially crossed into total bitch territory and I wasn't sure what that meant. I felt myself changing and growing more cynical, sarcastic, and brooding. I was becoming a master with words and hadn't fully decided if I would use my powers for good or evil.

* * *

Going to Dad's for the summer was becoming somewhat of an escape though I never knew what state he would be living in or what the climate of the household would be like. As I got older it became more bearable because Samantha relaxed quite a bit and we became close. Her daughters were older and off living their lives so perhaps it was easier for us to bond. I was older and taking better care of myself, so she no longer had to check me for lice or throw away all my clothes. We both loved shopping and would do it often though the woman could shop for eight hours straight without water or lunch. Sometimes I had to remind her that I might pass out if we didn't leave soon and hydrate. She was a like a machine on a total mission: to find that one awesome deal. It could be a handbag, blouse or anything, really. No hanger was left untouched on the sale rack. Occasionally she would pay full price for something, like when she bought me my first Swatch watch at Bloomingdale's. It was banana scented and I was so obsessed I sniffed my wrist for three weeks straight until the scent wore off.

Things were calmer at their house overall and I loved the fact that it was clean and beautiful. Samantha had a knack for making every room look spectacular. I can't recall one thing ever being out of place in their home. There wasn't even a single junk drawer. I always wondered where they kept stray screws or the Krazy Glue but never bothered to ask. The only thing that ever got out of control was Dad's drinking. He drank every day but normally it was beer and he handled it pretty well. His downfall was weekends when he went out with friends or when we went out to dinner as a family. Dad would have a drink before we left the house and several more at dinner. Martinis, Manhattans, wine, cordials—he was an all-out booze connoisseur. I was used to it except I became nervous when he got that glazed look in his eye knowing he would soon be behind the wheel attempting to drive us home. Every once in a while Samantha would convince him to let her drive, at which point he would pass out in the car with a lit cigarette and burn holes in the leather of whatever nice car they owned at the time. Oddly enough, she never bitched about it, at least not in my presence. She accepted Dad's drinking as part of him, like a double-chin or third nipple—just a part of who he was.

Even though Dad's drinking occasionally made me pray to Jesus (only in the car, really) I didn't experience much anger or frustration at their house, so I'm sure I came across as pleasant and maybe even sweet. I had buried all feelings about Dad kidnapping me and giving me a horrible start in life. Somehow the clothes, fun trips, sailboats, and so on obscured reality, but I hadn't even begun to process what had happened so I was blind. It was fun to have a dad with some money since growing up with Mom was such an experience of deprivation. Even after she married Larry, who did fairly well, I still felt poor because he constantly reminded me I wasn't his kid and he shouldn't have to buy me anything.

"Tell your rich dad to buy you shoes. He sure as hell doesn't pay much child support."

More than once he took my light bulb for three straight days because I had accidentally forgotten to turn off the light when I left my room. Dad never pulled any of that crap. He would just say, "Turn off your goddamned light," as if it were of no consequence but really he wouldn't even say that because everything that went on in the house was Samantha's responsibility. He was more like a guest there, to be waited on. Sure he would mow the grass on occasion but anything inside belonged to her. Her approach was stern but quiet. When I left dishes in the sink (her biggest pet peeve), instead of getting on to me she put them on my pillow so when I went to bed that night there they were, staring me in the face. I got the hint. I preferred that tactic to the yelling and screaming that Mom and Larry had become accustomed to. They had no reserve and certainly no desire to protect anyone's dignity. I guess that's why I attacked Mom's dignity. I was learning to speak their language.

Dad and Mikey yelled and fought often but for some reason it didn't bother me as much as when Mikey and Larry argued. Dad was a little softer and I also rationalized that Mikey was his son and he had more leverage to discipline. Dad did whip Mikey a few times with a belt but I felt even that was less offensive than Larry's total hatred and vitriol, which was getting progressively worse with each passing year. When Larry got mad he looked and sounded like the devil. His face would turn a deep reddish-purple which was like kryptonite to our little nervous systems.

Usually Mikey got the brunt of Larry's anger but when he wasn't around I was on the receiving end of the spit-spewing rages. Once we took a trip to Long Island to see my grandparents. As usual the trip didn't go well since Mom never got along with her parents after the kidnapping. They always ended up fighting. Grandpa complained about Mom's smoking even though she did it outside. Grandma always found something to bitch about too. It was clear the only reason they still communicated was because of me. Mom ate a lot of shit sandwiches in order for me to have grandparents. I think she was also still looking for their love and acceptance—something she never did get from them.

Mom had promised me that we would go to the local mall for new shoes while we were there. I was excited to shop at a fancy New York mall instead of the poor excuse for a local mall we had at home, which was still close to an hour away and only had a Kmart and JC Penney. I was thrilled to get some cool shoes that no one would have back at school and to see the latest styles. I had established my sense of style by that point and it was colorful and playful yet classy.

My favorite shoes were hot-pink suede cowboy booties I wish I'd kept to this day because I've never been able to find anything remotely like them since. I wore them with the pencil-thin Gloria Vanderbilt dark-blue jeans Samantha bought me and my oversized fuchsia sweatshirt, which was belted and hung off the shoulder. I always had enormous earrings that were cool but too heavy and made my ears sag a little though I didn't care one bit.

Walking through the mall was a little embarrassing since we were a huge brood. Mom was the slowest walker on the planet and she was still breast-feeding so she thought nothing of stopping in the middle of the walkway and whipping out a boob to feed my sister. I often walked a little ahead of the clan hoping no one thought I was with them. I felt like they were the Munsters and I was Marilyn—the only normal one.

This day was no different. I was always careful not to get too far ahead because Mom would yell "Sparrow, where are you?" as if I had been abducted all over again. But I was a little too excited about shoes and when I turned around to check for Mom I couldn't find her. I went into a slight panic and walked back so I could locate her, when out of the blue two hands grabbed my shoulders and started shaking me violently.

"DON'T YOU EVER WANDER OFF LIKE THAT AGAIN! DO YOU HEAR ME?"

I was stunned and couldn't speak. I tried to explain that I didn't mean to get so far ahead, that I was just excited, but no words would form. I became dizzy and lightheaded and thought I was going to pass out, especially when I realized that every single person in the vicinity had stopped what they were doing and were staring at me. Larry kept shaking and scream-spitting in my face but I blacked out and have no idea what he said. The last I recall was walking through the mall zombie-like, in shell shock. Needless to say there were no new shoes.

When Larry wasn't screaming in my face or ordering me around he was checking me out. He disgusted me on a fairly regular basis with comments about my clothing like, "That's a very sexy dress you are wearing," and "Do you have a bra on today?"

When I took a shower he'd sometimes pick the lock and say he had to pee even though we lived on a wooded acre and he could have either held it or pissed on a tree out back. The sound of him pissing right next to me when I was in the shower made my skin crawl. Then he'd flush and I'd get a big dose of hot water. Once he stood there after going and said, "You know, I could pull this shower curtain back whenever I want."

I reached over and grabbed a shampoo bottle—the only weapon I could think of but I was fairly certain I could beat the shit out of him with it if I needed to. I also considered squirting shampoo in his eyes then tearing down the shower curtain on top of him and making a run for it. In a split second I had my plan. Luckily I never had to execute. After a minute that seemed like a year he turned around and walked out, leaving me alone with my adrenaline and attack plan.

At night I moved my heavy dresser in front of my door so I felt safe when I slept. It took me more than a few minutes and I was screwed if I had to use the bathroom, but I did what I needed to in order to feel safe. I tried my best to shower when Larry was out of the house. I felt his eyes on me more and more and I had already been programmed to know what was coming. And it wasn't good.

Doug still came to visit from time to time and was always trying to hang out in my room. One time he sneaked in when I was still sleeping and crawled into bed with me.

"What the fuck? Get out!" I screamed and punched him anywhere I could make contact.

"Doug, come out of there," Mom said as if she were telling Mikey to get out of the cookie jar. No one seemed to mind that the experience took another five years off my life. I heard them in the kitchen laughing like it was some childish prank. It somehow became the family joke that Doug was into me. When I finally sprouted those rosebuds Larry took notice and grabbed my left one and said, "Look, Sparrow's growing boobs. Doug's really gonna want you now." Then he laughed as Mom looked away and went to find her cigarettes.

Larry continued to leer at me and Doug continued to defile me with his eyes, hands and tongue. More than once he walked past me when I was on the couch reading and grabbed me, holding me down and trying to kiss me. If I turned my head he would shove his tongue in my ear. I discovered a way to be numb to it all yet still have ninja-like reflexes and never hesitated to punch, kick, or slap anyone who entered my personal space bubble. I still have those reflexes today and have to be careful not to accidentally hit or punch anyone who gets too close to me or says something horribly offensive. I'm not always successful.

At some point I realized it would be better to be sexual with the boys at school in case my crazy family didn't leave me alone and I lost my virginity to my fat, disgusting step-uncle or worse my ignorant, mean bastard of a step-dad. I didn't know who the lucky guy would be; I just knew the longer I held onto my virginity the more likely someone horrible would take it. I saw how incest had affected Mom and some deep instinct told me to beware. It's one thing to have Disgusting Doug shove his tongue in your ear. It's another thing entirely for him to be shoving even bigger parts into harder to reach places. I knew if that happened I would be a goner —either completely crazy or in jail for homicide.

One of my classmates who lived down the street went to jail for shooting his step-dad with a .22. He got off the bus one day, walked into his trailer and blew the guy to bits. I was shocked but felt vindicated when I heard the news. I had experienced many fantasies of offing Larry, but I have never been a gun person. My daydreams involved drugging him with Mom's ground up prescription pills, tying him to a chair and torturing him in various ways, my favorite being sticking needles in his eyeballs. I knew that Richard's step dad deserved what he got as Richard was quiet, nice and never hurt a fly. I was only sad that he went to jail and wasn't coming out for a long time.

Mom and Larry were not an affectionate couple. I rarely saw them hug or kiss one another after the first year or so together. Sometimes they hung out on the same couch and watched a movie, but they never cuddled. Every once in a while they rubbed a "knot" out of each other's backs but it wasn't a lovey-dovey rub, it was always a perfunctory rub.

One of the most intimate exchanges I witnessed between the lovebirds was in the bathroom and quite by happenstance. The door was slightly ajar so I pushed it open, convinced no one was in there. I was wrong. Mom was on her knees perched on top of the toilet seat with her pants (and panties) at her ankles. There, under the fluorescent light was Mom's large, white ass right out in the open. The truth is it had gone from large to enormous after Doodie was born and it was saggy and peppered with cellulite. I hadn't seen Mom's naked ass in years and the sight of it is still etched in my psyche. What was even worse was the fact that Larry was on his knees too with his face up in Mom's full moon. At first I thought this was some bizarre sex act that would scar my eyeballs forever but then I realized what he was up to—he was popping a zit on Mom's fat pooper. Well, attempting to, anyway. "I don't see a head," I heard him say as I closed the door and fled from the most disgusting sight I had ever witnessed. There was never a more perfect time to swipe one of Mom's cigarettes and head out the back door to smoke and collect myself.

I skipped dinner that night, in part because I didn't want to look at either of them and in part because they had taken away my appetite. I thought for sure Mom would have said something later on, but as luck would have it they never even knew I was there. I certainly wasn't going to enlighten them.

The other intimate encounter I recall between Mom and Larry was another walk-in moment, but this time they were, in fact, shagging. It was one Saturday morning and my friend Dana had spent the night. We were hanging out at the breakfast bar in our pajamas when Mom came up to put some coffee on. She happened to be in a good mood, smiling and making jokes, which was odd because she hadn't even smoked or taken her meds yet.

"I'm gonna make breakfast, kids," she said as she headed back down the stairs to her bedroom. Mom only made breakfast two or three times a year so I was excited. Pancakes? French toast? I couldn't wait to have something other than the Total cereal Larry made us eat. He wouldn't even buy the kind with raisins because he thought it was too sugary. Gone were the days of Lucky Charms and Fruity Pebbles that we scarfed when we were on our own.

I waited and waited for Mom to come back upstairs but she never did. I finally decided to go check on her and see what was taking so long. Her bedroom door was open so I barged right in.

"Mom, what's for break..." I slammed the door and raced up the stairs. I didn't stop running until I reached my bedroom. Dana came running in after me.

"What's the matter?" she asked.

"My parents are getting it on!" I said, my head buried under a pillow.

"Eww. What did you see?"

I described how Larry was on top completely naked going at my mother like a jackhammer. I couldn't get his albino ass going up and down at a speed of one hundred miles an hour out of my head. I had no idea people shagged that way. It looked like something you would see in a wildlife documentary about hyenas or jackrabbits. It definitely didn't seem human.

A few minutes later Mom entered my room, all smiles. "Jeez, Sparrow, you almost ruined it." She laughed out loud.

Wow, so they kept going.

"Larry is embarrassed and won't come upstairs," she added.

I couldn't believe that I had seen part of him naked. Now I had seen both of their bare assess. It felt like a cruel joke from the universe. Why don't these people close doors? And lock them, too?

"I'm gonna make breakfast now," Mom said.

"Are you still hungry?" I asked Dana.

"Of course," she replied, unfazed. "Let's ask your Mom to make sausage," she added, and we both rolled on the floor in a total fit of hysterics.

Chapter 14

My tenth grade year was pretty uneventful at first. I was still getting grounded for my "smart mouth" so I spent a lot of time at home. I was shocked, however, when Mom said I could go with my friend Karen to see her relatives in Canada over winter break. Karen already had her license and we would drive on our own to stay with her grandmother in New Brunswick. That time of year was cold and snowy and we would be driving for eight hours but Mom didn't seem to mind. She knew Karen and trusted her. Perhaps she thought if I spent more time with her I would be more like her—respectful and accomplished.

Karen was an A+ student who won awards for everything and had a fan club made up of teachers and parents. She received preferential treatment from nearly everyone, and people felt sorry for her because her mom had died of a brain aneurysm a few years before. It was indeed a tragedy.

Karen was an enticing person to spend time with, but not for the reason everyone was thinking. Karen was fun, like *super* fun. Karen was a druggie. She was also a Deadhead, and the two usually went hand in hand in my school. Every time I got in the car with Karen she lit up. She smoked cigarettes too, but I'm talking weed and her favorite—hashish. I'm not sure where Karen got her drugs but she always had them and never seemed to be ashamed about it. She had nearly every Dead bootleg and told me which show and which generation we were listening to. She quickly converted me and I spent lots of time alternating between Jerry Garcia and Robert Smith because I couldn't completely abandon my mod roots.

Karen dressed in flowing skirts, which hid her hairy legs. I couldn't figure out why she couldn't be one of those Deadheads that shaved but I thought it rude to ask. I became the stylish Deadhead, with my tight-fitting tie-dye t-shirts and sexy jeans with holes. I hated wearing flats but I found a few pairs I could get by with. I couldn't forgo makeup like Karen and her friends but I went for the understated look with muted tones that were a shift from the purple and green eye shadows I had grown fond of. I tried to stay away from blues since they didn't do much for me but I rocked purple mascara in those days, just not when I was with Karen. I kind of liked having a new style to gravitate toward and had found a lovely long, brown paisley skirt with giant pockets on each side I wore frequently, if for no other reason than I could fit a beer in each pocket, kind of like Frank and his motorcycle boots.

"I can't believe my mom is letting me go with you," I told Karen one day at school. "We're going to have a blast!" She reminded me that many people spoke French up there and that I should brush up. Her family was French so she was pretty fluent, but I was only in my second year so I needed to practice. That wasn't a problem because I was in love with the French language and culture and I wanted nothing more than to be French myself. And the good news was I was great at it. I picked up the language quickly and it was my only A in school, mainly because it was the only class I did the homework in and studied for. I didn't see history or geometry as skills for the future but I knew French would be.

I also loved French literature and just because I wasn't reading about the Civil War doesn't mean I wasn't reading. I loved books. Actually, I worshiped books. I read constantly and when I was able to start reading in French I was all the more excited. Mom went to the library sales and bought me the old, worn classics they were getting rid of. I had cut my teeth on the likes of Freud, Adler and other experts in the field of psychology after Mom would read them for school and now I had worked my way up to the French authors like Camus and Sartre.

I found a home in existentialism. I had frequent daydreams of one day moving to Paris, wearing black cashmere turtlenecks with three-quarter length sleeves, and eloquently discussing *Huis Clos* as I sipped tea and smoked cigarettes in a long cigarette holder like Audrey Hepburn. Of course I would be sporting a black beret and cherry red lips, like any stylish French girl. But it wasn't just about the clothes for me. It was the way of life. French people were passionate, intelligent and beautiful. They were sophisticated and I'm sure no French girl had to live with a giant sign in her front yard that said FREE PUPIES because her step-father didn't know how to spell the word puppies correctly.

I fell in love with the existentialist movement and philosophy— that you are born alone and die alone. Many might find it somber but for me it was liberating. Since I couldn't count on anyone in my family anyway, I decided to revel in my solitude and create my own reality. My plan was to move to Paris as soon as I graduated college and get a job so I could pay for all the café time and cigarettes I'd be smoking there. It seemed brilliant.

In the meantime I was okay with wearing tie-dyes so I could spend time with Karen. I was never going to trip on acid or do the new concert drug X she raved about, but I still loved being with her. She represented a freedom to me that was appealing in that it was possible to live out loud and still have your shit together, at least somewhat. I was taking notes.

Mom sent me off to Canada with a hundred dollars and a surprise hug. "Have fun touring all the basilicas," she called out as she waved us off. She was being unusually supportive and I wondered if perhaps Dr. Robertson had changed her meds. Karen had told her that we were going to Montreal to do some sight-seeing and she seemed excited for us. I wonder if she had thought back to her own honeymoon there, but I didn't ask. No sense throwing Mom off a cliff for no good reason.

Karen did all the driving because I didn't even have a permit at that time. Back then you could get a driver's license at fifteen and she was one of the first in our class to have one. We drove and toked and listened to hours and hours of the Dead. "This album is called Terrapin Station, and it's my favorite," she said. She knew so much and I took it all in. She educated me on Jerry, Bob, Phil, Pigpen and I can't remember who else. I decided I liked Jerry's voice the most, and "Uncle John's Band" became my favorite Dead tune. It spoke to me in the first verse, because the first days were my hardest days too. I also related to a verse later in the song since my motto had been "don't tread on me" for as long as I could remember. It felt like my anthem. I asked Karen to play it over and over until she told me it was driving her bananas so we switched tapes.

Grandma's house was tiny and quaint, with dainty floral wallpaper and light-blue carpet. I could tell it hadn't been updated in years but that made it all the more charming. Our room was upstairs which was nice because it gave us some privacy and our own bathroom. Granny didn't speak a word of English but I was able to exchange pleasantries with my beginner's French. She seemed excited to have us there, but she was old and didn't get around well, so she didn't spend much time with us.

We turned in early the night we got there and by the next day we were ready to go. Karen took me all around her stomping grounds; Edmundston, New Brunswick. We didn't tour any basilicas but I met a few of her cousins and we all hung out and drank Alpine beer, which Karen said was better than Labatt, the other popular Canadian beer. I was crushing on her older cousin Andre. He was about twenty-three and had thick, black hair, big muscles and a smile that reminded me of a glacier. He wasn't at all interested in me, which was indeed unfortunate because he was the most exotic man I had ever laid eyes on.

Later that night we decided to go to our first discotheque— a supposedly cool out-of-the-way place called L'arc en Ciel, which means The Rainbow. I asked if it was wise because it was a Sunday night and I had a feeling clubs were lame on Sundays, but Karen's cousin Alana insisted it would still be fun. She was also a sophomore and shared her brother Andre's dark, wavy hair. She was the only cousin who wanted to go dancing with us.

The club really was out of the way— we're talking dirt road. I was getting nervous, thinking it was going to be some local hole in the wall, but I was pleasantly surprised when we walked in. It was modern, with giant TV screens and a dance floor complete with the standard disco ball. No one checked IDs since we were seriously underage and the bouncer told us we were in for a real treat. He spoke in French and Karen had to translate for me but we still had no idea what that meant.

"Perhaps drinks are two for one," I said, trying to be positive. Things were more expensive in Canada and I wanted to make sure my hundred dollars lasted the entire week.

We found a table and the three of us sat down. We all ordered Alpine beers and engaged in your average girl talk. Karen and I were single but Alana was kind of dating someone she really liked, so she wasn't looking to meet boys. There weren't many people in the club but it was early and I was hoping it would pick up. Cartoons were playing on the big screens and the music was good, mostly eighties mod like Erasure and New Order. I was happy.

As the night wore on more people showed up. I couldn't believe how many good-looking guys were in this club. Where did they come from? Most of them looked like GQ models. We were taking in the eye candy when I noticed two men across the bar making out like crazy.

"Oh my God, Karen, look!" I tugged her shirt to get her attention.

"What the hell?" She was stunned. We had a good look around, and noticed we were the only three girls in the club. We were completely engulfed by gay men.

"Alana! You took us to a gay bar!" Karen said to her cousin.

"I swear this isn't typically a gay bar," she responded, shocked.

I had developed a pretty good relationship with our waiter since Karen had suggested I flirt with him to get free drinks. His name was Daniel and he didn't speak English but it was okay because after several drinks my French improved. He was twenty-five (I asked) and was wearing a three-piece suit with a thin aqua tie. He had brown hair and a mustache that made me think of Jimmy Buffet's song "Pencil Thin Mustache" though his was thick, unlike the song. I wasn't really into mustaches but he had stopped charging us for drinks so I was fine with leading him on.

I asked him if it was a gay club and he said only on Sundays. Of course that was my luck. My first disco experience and the boys want to dance with each other. Daniel told me not to worry because there was a big surprise coming. *What the hell is this surprise?* I wondered. I was getting impatient.

By this time the Alpines were kicking in along with the tequila shots Daniel brought us and I full-on made out with our waiter. Truthfully I wasn't really hot for him but I wanted to be the hero of the night and score free drinks. I decided I liked having that kind of power. Was it really that easy?

Before I knew it the surprise came. A few men went over to the corner and pulled a giant stage out of the wall. It was kind of like a Murphy bed only it was a stage. It happened to be directly in front of our table, so we had front row seats. Just then the music changed and I noticed they were no longer playing cartoons on the big screens. It had switched over to porn. Very. Gay. Porn. The men at the other tables were yelling and whistling like they knew what was coming. It was like being at the circus, waiting for the next act, having no idea if it would be lions, tigers, bears or elephants.

What is this all about? It took longer than it should have to figure it out. Out of nowhere a policeman got on stage and began dancing. At first, I was nervous since we were underage and I was afraid of cops to begin with. *What if we get busted in a foreign country? Would Granny know how to bail us out?* These thoughts and more were racing through my head. It took me more than a minute to realize he wasn't an actual police officer, just playing one on stage. A very naughty police officer, who was taking his uniform off piece by piece.

"What the fuck?" I whispered loudly in Karen's ear. My horror quickly turned to laughter when I caught Karen's eye and saw her face. We both cracked up, not just from the alcohol but also due to the fact that we had gotten ourselves into a pile of shit.

Our naughty police officer turned criminal when he flung his G-string across the room at one of the tables filled with drooling men, a table that included Alana's history teacher.

"Oh my God what if he sees me?" she panicked.

"Trust me, he has more to worry about than you," Karen said between fits of laughter. Just then one of the managers approached our table.

"Ladeez, pleez do not leff at zee men on stage, they vil looze their rections."

"We are *so* sorry," I replied, pinching myself hard to keep from laughing. I kicked both girls under the table to get them to stop too. I wasn't interested in naughty police officer's hard penis but it was kind of like a train wreck I couldn't drag myself away from, so I wasn't ready to get kicked out.

After the officer's show was over we clapped and hooted, right along with the gays. *We are here, we may as well enjoy it,* was the sentiment. Plus, I knew I was getting a tremendous education in this place, though I couldn't quite decide how I would use it later in life.

Our next fabulous dancer was a slightly older man dressed as a construction worker. He didn't quite have the moves of naughty officer but his pecs were enormous as were other important parts so we clapped hard for him too. We weren't about to lose any dollar bills to these guys but we still wanted to show our support. After he was finished Pencil Thick stopped at our table to whisper in my ear. "Pour vous, cherie." I instantly felt blood rush to my face. It was one thing to make out with Pencil Thick, but I really didn't want to see his junk. Quel horreur!

I had to admit, Pencil Thick had some serious moves. I'm sure he laid it on extra thick for me, especially since he jumped off the stage and danced freak-ass naked right in front of me. Karen and Alana had degraded into woo-girls, I was beyond red and the gays were beyond pissed. I'm sure they felt like we were en-crotching on their territory and we were all getting the stink eye. I did my best to get into the show, remembering all the free drinks we had gotten throughout the night.

As soon as his number was over my instincts told me it was time to leave. A moment later I happened to glance at one of the big screens to see a horrifying clip of a young boy going down on an old man. Yes, we needed to get the hell out of there.

"Karen, I need to use the bathroom and then can we please leave?" It was getting late anyway and we had certainly experienced everything we needed to at L'arc by now.

"Sure thing," she said as she collected our purses. I darted into the ladies room, heading to the very last stall which I had a habit of doing. As I went to close the stall door someone forcefully swung it open and stepped inside the stall with me. It was Pencil Thick.

"You owe me," he said in English. So, he spoke English after all. "Blow me." He pushed the top of my head down hard which caused me to fall to my knees. He was sporting a canary yellow G-string that he pulled down with his other hand. All of a sudden I was one hundred percent sober and went into pure survival mode. Being tiny and flexible I crawled under all three stalls on my hands and knees until I reached the last one. In a flash I was up and out the bathroom door.

"Karen, run!" I screamed as I sprinted for the door. She and Alana had all of our things so we ran out the front door, never stopping until we got to the car.

"What happened?" she asked, out of breath by the time she got into the driver's seat.

"Our waiter assaulted me in the bathroom. He tried to make me blow him. We need to get out of here!" It was December and below zero and the roads were ice and snow covered. Karen got the car started but it needed to warm up so we couldn't leave right away. I was eyeing the door, making sure no one was after us. After a minute or so Karen backed out and turned the car too abruptly plowing us into a snow bank on the side of the road.

"Sonofabitch!" she cried, as she tried to back up. The wheels were spinning but we were going nowhere. I kept thinking, *Oh my god we are screwed.* I pictured Pencil Thick putting his suit back on to come find us. Alana and I got out and tried to push. We were in heels but we're Northern girls so we can be tough when we need to be. We pushed and pushed and nothing. A few minutes later some angels arrived in a black pickup truck. And by angels I mean three gay men dressed head to toe in red leather. Red leather pants, red leather jackets and I swear they were all wearing red leather Reebok high tops. They looked just like something out of a Romantics video. They didn't speak any English but the three of them were able to push our car out of the bank in the span of a few short minutes.

"Merci bien!" we called out to them as we got the hell out of there. It took a good solid five minutes before any of us felt comfortable laughing again. We laughed because the whole night was a freak show, but we also laughed because we were finally safe.

That happened to be one eventful winter. Jess began dating a guy named Bob who was twenty-three and looked like a younger version of Billy Idol— hair color, bone structure, he had it all. He lived about an hour away in his mom's basement which was set up like a giant one-room apartment with its own kitchen and a separate entrance. We hung out there from time to time though it was awkward because after a few hours of drinking and watching movies Jess and Bob would start getting it on in his bed which normally wouldn't have bothered me except his bed was four feet away from the couch and Jess was a screamer. At least the bed was behind the couch so I could watch TV and turn the volume up loud to drown out the grunts and groans.

One time after they were finished Bob asked if I wanted to "cuddle" with them. "I'm good, thanks," I yelled over the blaring television without even turning around. I much preferred to be the third wheel.

Bob was friends with an older guy named Fred who owned a tiny cabin in the mountains not far from Bob's house. It was more like a glorified one-room shack that had a double bed and a single chair in it. I wasn't a fan of partying at Fat Fuckin' Fred's (his real nickname) because I hated peeing outside and there was no privacy if you wanted to go make out with a boy, but I was always outvoted.

Fred had a semi-adopted son named Sam who was my age and was almost always at the cabin when I got there. He was sweet and had a giant crush on me but unfortunately he was at the peak of his Peter Brady phase. I'm not sure what had happened but his face reminded me of a Picasso during his cubist years; nothing was where it was supposed to be. I tried to keep it platonic with poor

Sam but his sweetness along with the alcohol made me give in to him more than once. It was always dark inside the cabin and after four beers and two shots if I looked at him sideways and cut my eyes just so he became adorable in a Muppet-like way. Sooner or later I went for it and kissed him a few times though it was nowhere near a make-out session due to the lack of privacy. Most of the time Sam and I talked or played cards and I was grateful.

"Fred invited us to the cabin," Bob said one night when we were hanging at his place. It was a cold, snowy Saturday evening and there were no parties that we knew of, though I didn't really enjoy parties with Bob's friends because they were all older and into heavier drugs. A few weeks prior we had gone to one where a guy offered me something called "rush" that was some liquid in a tiny vial you were supposed to inhale. I politely declined, especially since the guy who offered it was stumbling around and seemed like he lost one too many brain cells. Several other people at that party were sitting around the coffee table inhaling lines of coke and rubbing it on their gums, which freaked me out even more. I much preferred my high school parties where people were dancing and doing shots of peppermint schnapps. That, I could handle.

I wanted to stay inside where it was warm but once again I was outvoted.

"Come on, we'll just go for a few hours," Jess said as she pulled me off the couch. "We'll stop and get you your favorite wine coolers." I was thankful Bob was old enough to buy all our alcohol. He usually paid for it too, which was nice. He had a full time job in construction and did pretty well for his age; he also didn't have to pay rent. I had never seen anyone do drugs other than weed at Fred's so it did feel a little safer.

"Okay, I'll go," I said.

Things were status quo at the cabin. I was happy with my Bartles & Jaymes original flavor wine coolers that Dad had introduced me to one summer on the lake. Fred had a nice fire going in the wood stove and the temperature in the cabin had to be at least ninety degrees. Sam and I were sitting on the floor playing gin. Bob and Jess were lounging on the bed laughing and playing Steve Miller on the stereo. Fred lit a blunt and we all got high. A perfect evening.

"Sparrow, do you want a beer?" Bob asked a while later. I was still sitting crossed-legged on the floor playing cards. I was winning and was focused on the game. Bob was standing over me to my left when he shoved a beer in my face.

"No thanks," I replied as I turned my head to look up at him. That's when I saw it. "What the hell?" I cried as I turned my head and covered my face with my arm. Everyone was laughing hysterically, except for me and Sam. Bob got me. "Cover that shit up!" I yelled, stunned that he was standing there completely naked with his junk in my face. Just then I looked around and noticed that everyone was completely naked except for Sam and me. They were still laughing uncontrollably, delighted that they had punked me. I'm sure the look on my face alone was enough to send them into hysterics, especially since I was the goodie-goodie of the bunch, which wasn't saying much.

"Sparrow, come sit on my lap," Fred said, laughing as he patted his right leg. I still thank Jesus that Fat Fuckin' Fred really was pretty fat and his pregnant gut was so large it covered any view of cock and balls. I glanced over at Jess who was sitting stark naked on the bed, her enormous saggy tatas staring at me, trying to make eye contact.

"Come on, Sparrow, take your clothes off. We're going outside to take showers." Someone had come up with the bright idea of heating water on the stove, going outside in the snow and dumping the hot water over each other, which sounded like the absolute definition of hell to me. Any buzz I had completely vanished at that moment and I shot up as if my ass was on fire.

"You people are fucking crazy!" I screamed as I dashed out the door and ran for my life. Jess's car was parked at the bottom of the drive and I had never been so happy to see it. I opened the passenger door and dove in head first, then locked all four doors. I didn't have a coat or keys but I considered myself safe for the moment. Within a matter of minutes Jess got dressed and came out to coax me back in. When I wouldn't let her in the car she started banging on the window.

"Sparrow, stop overreacting. You're going to freeze if you stay out here. Come back inside."

"Go away, you freak! I'm fine, go have your fun. I'm staying here until you're ready to go home." It was my only choice. Sam didn't drive and there was no way I was going anywhere near the other guys.

Jess went back inside and Sam came out. He pleaded and cajoled but I wouldn't even look at him. I considered him guilty by association because he didn't bat an eye when everyone was naked. He was probably just as blind-sided as me, but I couldn't take my chances. He was on my shit list now, too.

Jess and Bob did do the shower thing with Fred on the front porch of the cabin. I didn't stare, but couldn't help noticing. Why anyone would want to get naked with a fat fifty-year-old geezer was beyond me. Did I mention he was also beaten with an ugly stick? Who knows, maybe he was Sam's real dad after all.

I had other friends at school, such as Callie and Dana, but I still spent the most time with Jess. She lived in a big house with almost no parental supervision, and she had her own car. Her parents owned a lake house right across the street from their main house with a pontoon boat we could use whenever we wanted. Jessica had evolved into a total partier. She drank and smoked nearly every day and frequently stole weed from her parents that we would smoke whenever we had the chance. I was happy to be her sidekick because it got me out of my shabby house filled with yelling and cigarette smoke.

Jess never had any chores at her house so we were free to do whatever we wanted. Her two favorite pastimes were eating and sex, in that order. At some point in junior high Jess developed bulimia, probably because her mom was always on her to lose ten pounds. Jess could easily put down thirty thousand calories in one sitting. She'd eat and eat and eat, then excuse herself to go hurl in the bathroom. The longer we were friends the less she hid it, until she would puke her guts out right in front of me.

We got movie tickets for the opening night of *The Lost Boys*. Jess insisted on eating her favorite combination of popcorn and M&M's and drinking beers we had smuggled inside our coats. Immediately after the movie she had to go to the bathroom. As I was peeing she was in the next stall puking up everything she had just scarfed. The movie theater manager, this old guy, was banging on the door to the ladies' room yelling at us to come out. He probably thought we were drunk. Jess was a loud puker but she was quick and made it seem easy. She knew exactly where to stick her fingers to make herself vomit within seconds. I never lectured or scolded her and even got used to the sounds and smells, helping her clean up after she was done. We never had one discussion about it that I can remember, except for her saying she was sick of being fat. Her weight would fluctuate quite a lot, depending on how much she binged. She had zero self-control.

I never overate; probably because I was too busy smoking. I was stick thin and wanted to stay that way. I ate plenty of junk food, just not in large quantities. Jess was jealous of how I looked in a bathing suit and once told me she had tried to sabotage all of my relationships with boys because she hated how thin I was. I had no idea but I pieced it together after asking some questions and realized she had broken up all the relationships I was happy in, including the one with the hottest boy in school, Phil Nace.

I had seen Phil in the local pizza place when I was in eighth grade. He was a grade ahead of me, already in high school. He had longish dark-blond hair, the biggest dimples you ever saw, and was wearing a gray trench coat. I was smitten and had promised myself that one day I would date that boy. Sophomore year it happened. We had become friends through friends and he asked me out. I was ecstatic to be dating *the* Phil Nace. School days were filled not with caring about my subjects, but daydreaming about Dimples and what he was doing. He had a harem of girls following him wherever he went and I was always worried. I wasn't about to sleep with him any time soon so I was scared some other girl would lure him away. It had happened before with other guys.

Jess and I went to a party one night at a pond in the middle of nowhere. We were usually at every party unless I was grounded. Things were fun until I sneaked off into the woods to pee. Little did I know I was being followed. Steve Herman, a junior on the wrestling team, tackled me from behind and we rolled around on the ground.

"Get off me!" I screamed, to no avail. He pinned me to the ground and his face was in my face. He was trying to make out with me, only he was super drunk and slobbering all over me and clearly not understanding that I wasn't interested. "Get off me, I have a boyfriend!" I managed to yell after pushing his face off of mine. "I'm dating Phil Nace!"

"What? Oh, hey, I'm sorry about that. Phil's my friend," he said as he got up and brushed himself off. Suddenly he didn't seem quite so drunk. "Good luck with Phil, he's a great guy," Steve mumbled as he walked back to the party, leaving me sitting on the ground picking grass out of my hair.

When I returned to the party I pulled Jess away to tell her. "Oh my God he's so disgusting!" she said, horrified. "Let's get out of here." We got in her car and smoked a few bowls, singing along to Steve Miller and laughing about the whole thing. She was supportive and tried to take my mind off it. These things happened from time to time and were definitely party hazards. Jess never said no to any boy that came onto her, I think because she was so happy to get the attention. I was rather choosy. He had to be cute and he had to have an edge. I wasn't really into preppy boys. I liked the guys with wallets on chains, facial scars from fights, bumps on noses or even freckles. They had to have *something*.

I had all but forgotten about the Steve incident Monday at school when Dimples broke up with me. I was stunned.

"But why?" I asked.

"Ask your friend Jess," he said as he walked away from me. At lunch, I made a bee-line for Jess and told her what happened.

"I have no idea why he would say that." Dimples later told me that Jess told him I had hooked up with Steve at the party. My best friend betrayed me. And it wasn't the first time. I was angry. I tried to tell him what really happened but he didn't believe me. It didn't matter anyway, because he was already on to the next girl. I just had to get over him.

I forgave Jess because my alternative was to sit in my own house with my crazy family. I willingly sold my soul to escape my life, knowing she was becoming the friend from hell.

I did occasionally spend some time with a friend from work named Gwen. We met at my first job which was working in a store that sold suitcases and umbrellas. We were the same age yet she was much worldlier. She had a license and her own car and her mom let her come and go as she pleased. She never got grounded or had to check in. She used to pick me up for work since my house was on the way and I was grateful since I had no license and Mom wasn't keen on driving me to work forty-five minutes one way. I tried to pay her gas money but she never took it.

Gwen was a take-charge person. She was quickly promoted at work and typically in charge of me. She kept me busy and I made sure to follow her every instruction. She worked hard but she also played hard. Like, *really* hard.

Hanging out with Gwen was an experience. The first time I walked into her bedroom I stared wide-eyed at the posters on her wall— full-frontal tear outs from *Playgirl* magazine. I never even knew such a magazine existed. She did, and had plastered her room with dicks. Dicks of all shapes and sizes.

"Your mom lets you hang this stuff?" I asked, still in shock.

"She can't stop me." Gwen's dad had died when she was young and it was just her and her mother. I think her mom had given up any parenting efforts years before. Gwen smoked cigarettes in her home, used weed daily, and, oh yeah, worshiped the devil.

"Yeah, I'm a Satanist," she said one day when I asked what her upside down star necklace was about.

"Why do you worship the devil?"

"It's a long story."

"Don't you believe in God?"

"If there was a God, he wouldn't have taken my father." I didn't know how to argue with that one so I didn't. I decided we could be friends as long as she didn't want to drink my blood or try to get me to convert. Even though my life was far from roses I still considered Jesus my homeboy and I wanted nothing to do with black cloaks and animal sacrifice. But there was something trustworthy about Gwen. She was the only person who always looked out for me. Plus, who knew? If things got any worse at home I might need her to cast a spell of some kind. I just knew she would if I asked.

I'm not sure what Gwen saw in me. Perhaps she liked having a fan club with one member. Many people, well, girls in particular, didn't care for her. She was intense and intimidating if she didn't like you. Dana worked with us briefly but left because she and Gwen fought constantly. I had never witnessed it but Gwen told me that she had been in her fair share of cat fights and I believed her. I also believed she never lost a single one.

One night Gwen and I were driving down Main Street when she pulled into the local gas station. I thought for sure she was stopping for smokes. It didn't matter if she was underage, for some reason she never got carded. She got out of the car and popped the trunk. In a flash Gwen had grabbed a wooden bat and started beating the old blue truck next to us. She really went to town, busting out headlights, tail lights and both side mirrors. She cracked the windshield. I sat there stunned, as she just kept at it. I had never seen her so wild-eyed.

Not sure of what else to do I lit a cigarette and stared straight ahead as I knew better than to interfere in any way. I cracked the window for air but also to be a little closer to her, seeing as how the truck was parked on my side. When she had sufficiently beaten it to death she calmly put the bat back in the trunk, then hopped in the driver's seat.

"Okay, Sparrow, where to next?" she asked as if nothing had happened. We screeched out of the parking lot.

"What was that all about?" I was confused, yet impressed. The girl was strong.

"That was Darren's truck, the mother-fucker who cheated on me. Fuck that prick," she laughed. I was too cautious to laugh, wondering who had witnessed what just happened. The Main Street cops were always driving around looking to bust teens for any little thing.

"Gwen, there are cops everywhere, what if someone saw you?"

"Oh, like this cop?" she giggled and she pulled into the rival Handi-Mart across the street and a few blocks south. There was a police car parked off to the side of the store. "Come on, follow me," she said as she parked the car and darted out. I was still struggling to get my seat belt off when she opened the rear passenger door of the cop car and jumped in. Trusting her completely, I got in next to her, thinking I had to be in an alternate universe. *Am I really getting into a cop car?* I had spent my whole life hating "pigs" thanks to Frank. I remembered when a cop came to the house because Frank had gone to the dump after business hours and had left our garbage bags neatly stacked outside the gate.

"Young lady, are your parents home?" the rather heavy officer said.

"Mom, another cop is here," I yelled as I went to my room, leaving him standing at the door. I left my door cracked so I could eavesdrop, like always. The officer had gone through the trash and traced it back to our house. On top of a fine we also got the garbage back. I think that was the day when the huge trash pile on our deck first appeared.

"Farley, this is my friend Sparrow," Gwen said as she introduced me to the officer in the driver's seat.

"Hiya Sparrow." Farley had a reputation for busting my friends on a regular basis. I hated his name but what I hated more was how people with a Maine accent said it, though I hated how Mainers said everything. The accent was like nails on a chalkboard to me, and what was worse was you never knew who would have it. Farley's accent was hideous, but all cops were hideous anyway so it really didn't matter.

"Whatcha ladies doin' tonight? Owt ridin around, eh?"

"Ayuh, lookin' for a pahty," Gwen said, slathering on the accent and lighting up a joint. *Oh my fucking word is she really smoking weed in a cop car?* She handed it to me and for the first time ever I declined. I wasn't quite ready for juvie yet. There were too many boys to date. Farley didn't say a word about the spliff and after bantering for a few minutes we were back in Gwen's car and on our way. If she wasn't my hero before she definitely was after that encounter.

"How do you know that cop?" I asked.

"I know lots of people in this town, Sparrow," was all she would say. I wondered if she had slept with him but I didn't dare ask. Sometimes she would share intimate details and other times not. She did tell me once, "I never kiss on the lips. It's too personal." I thought that was strange since I loved making out with boys. "Fucking is fine but never kissing. It's so gross!" she said, making a face that looked like she had just sucked a lemon. I thought lips were way sexier than dicks but all you had to do was step into Gwen's room to tell she disagreed.

Chapter 15

Growing up in the sticks it became harder and harder to find role models. Sure I worshiped Cindy Crawford, Demi Moore and Molly Ringwald, but they weren't really teaching me much about how to be a strong, confident woman. I did learn how to dress impeccably and how to chase boys, but I was looking for more.

That all changed when I came home from school one day to find Mom watching something called the Oprah Winfrey Show. I don't recall exactly what the show was about but I was captivated. This woman was strong, passionate, caring and *smart*. She knew how to command an audience and really challenge people. I was instantly hooked.

I started making it a routine practice to grab a snack and plop in front of the TV after school for Oprah time. I didn't know much about her personally, but I had a feeling she had to work hard to get her own show. I just knew she probably had to fight off a perverted uncle or two herself. She seemed to have a personality that said, "I'm nice but don't fuck with me" and I could relate. I found out Ms. Winfrey didn't have any kids, and I thought about how much fun it would be if she adopted me. I bet she didn't chain-smoke, or take pills to get through the day, or check out when things got stressful. I knew she handled things like a boss, and I wanted to be like her. Mom liked her too, but Mom didn't show any desire to get her shit together. Instead, she was content plugging into someone else who had it together for an hour a day.

It wasn't long before I was dressing more like Oprah and less like a wannabe supermodel. Well, at least some of the time. I got my hands on a few power suits and wore them to school on occasion. My skirt hem got longer and longer. I even started doing more homework. I decided I could be successful one day and needed to act the part.

Not too long after I discovered my new hero I went to visit Mom's parents for a few days. Even though I was a teen I still enjoyed being there and eating Grandma's French toast, but diabetes was slowly taking Grandma's eyesight and she'd often mistake the oregano for the cinnamon. When I complained she would dismiss it and tell me to pretend it was pizza.

One afternoon I was flipping through the channels and happened to find Oprah on. Score! I was only a few minutes into the show when Grandpa walked in and noticed what I was watching.

"Get that jungle bunny program off my TV!" he yelled, waving his hand in the air, swatting those hornets again.

Oh no. Here comes that rage I try so hard to keep down. In an instant I was transported back to that moment with the little girl on her pink bicycle who wanted to play. I didn't know how to handle that back then but I was older and wiser now and let's face it, a whole lot angrier.

"What did you say?" I yelled, standing up from the couch and moving toward him.

"You heard me. Get that off of there!"

I can't explain what happened next, except to say that perhaps Grandpa Johnny was on the receiving end of my wrath for everyone who ever had ever hurt me to my core. It was one thing to pick on me, but another to defile someone I was so fond of.

"Excuse me, do you think you're white or something?" A voice came out of me that was dark and growling and sounded like a cross between a demon and a troll. I sounded just like Larry.

"Have you looked in the mirror lately? Because you're not!" Grandpa Johnny prided himself on his dark complexion and spent hours in the sun tanning during the summer months. He even doused himself with pure baby oil so he could get extra dark and crispy. No one would have thought him Caucasian.

"Guess what, Asshole? Most people would mistake you for a sand nigger!" Grandpa froze. So did I. I couldn't believe I had just said that, but then again I could. I don't recall where I had ever heard such a derogatory term, though I had heard Dad say the *n*-word on more than one occasion. In all honesty it's possible a ghost or spirit entered my body and hurled those deplorable words. All I knew was I didn't regret them.

I had never seen Grandpa Johnny so stunned or speechless. Typically it was he who yelled insults at everyone. I had never once seen someone truly stand up to him. He looked right through me and left the room. I don't know where he went but he didn't come back for a long time.

Oddly enough Grandma was absent through all this. I'm sure she heard every word since the house was small, but she never brought it up. I quietly resumed my spot on the plastic-covered sofa and continued watching my Oprah show, feeling a newfound strength and unexpected calm. I vowed to never put up with that kind of bullshit ever again. Even if he was someone I loved so much, he still crossed a line and it wasn't okay.

* * *

Grandma's spare room had built-in bookshelves on two walls that were crammed with every paperback romance novel ever printed. Nearly all of them had some scantily clad man and woman on the front in a desperate embrace and the covers were creased and well-worn since Grandma folded them over when she read them.

I never read Grandma's books because I always had my own and they had never appealed to me anyway, which didn't make sense since I liked boys so much. I think I was turned off by the cheesy covers and I wasn't at all attracted to long-haired Fabio types wearing billowy pirate shirts. I didn't read much fiction anyway, especially since Jess had insisted I read *Pet Cemetery* which gave me nightmares for six months of every animal I had ever owned that was dead. No thanks.

Once when I was getting ready to go home after visiting my grandparents Grandma noticed I had finished my book and wouldn't have anything to read on the nine-hour bus ride. "Wait a sec," she said, disappearing into the spare room. When she returned she was holding a thick book with a white cover. "Here you go," she said as she tucked it into my backpack. "It's a little steamy but I think you can handle it." I wondered what kind of book it was since there weren't two people about to have sex on the cover. Grandma also packed a few crossword puzzles for me which I loved ever since she taught me how to do them. Plenty to keep me busy, though I didn't mind the long ride unless I sat next to some drunk guy who fell asleep and leaned his head on my shoulder, which had happened more than once. I was always too timid to push them off and so I would just sit there and let them use me as a pillow even though they sometimes drooled or smelled like cheese.

I was lucky on this particular ride as I had the row to myself so I took my shoes off, got comfy, and dug into the book. *Chances*, by Jackie Collins. Right away it was a page-turner. The book was about a gorgeous, Italian lady boss who wore *Vogue*-worthy clothes and told people what to do. I was instantly hooked. It was riveting and made time fly by as I was learning about the main character,

Lucky, and her family. *I'm meant to read this book,* I thought. And then I got to the "steamy" part. Oh. Ooh. What...? People do that? And that too? Grandma was wrong. It wasn't steamy, it was *scandalous.* I had no idea even fictional people behaved in this manner. I was so shocked I don't think I blinked for four pages, and I was blazing through those pages on a mission. This was my first true birds and bees lesson. I thought I'd learned a lot in eighth grade health class when I was taught about ovulation and had to feel the fake boob to try and find the lump, which I never could find. This made that stuff feel like baby talk. This was X-rated.

I read and read and never did get to those crossword puzzles. I was a good two-hundred pages into the book before I arrived home. I realized later that I had creased the cover page just like Grandma did because I didn't want anyone to see the title and know I was reading smut, at least I was pretty sure that's what it was called. I was intrigued by the book but a little disappointed in Grandma. This woman, who hummed while she cooked and sewed clothes for me was reading this stuff. I refused to relegate Grandma to my growing list of pervs but I was more than a little disenchanted.

* * *

That was the year to stand up to grandfathers. Punky wasn't close to Mom's parents but she was close to her grandparents on Frank's side. Arthur and Lorraine still lived in that old house in New Hampshire and came to pick her up for the weekend every few months to spend time with her. Mom liked it because they would buy her things she needed like school clothes or toys for her birthday and that was more money Mom could spend on cigarettes or send to Jesus. To be fair, I think Mom had stopped sending money to the televangelists because one (or more) had well-publicized affairs and she had recently become a feminist because she had to read some book called *The Women's Room* for a college class she was taking. I think she started donating money to some organization she was in called the Coalition. She had taken us to one of their meetings but it turned out to be a potluck event and I never determined what their oh-so important cause was.

I decided I hated feminism, not because I loved boys but because it gave Mom a great excuse to stop doing the tiny bit of housework that she did. In addition to all the terrible things that happened in her past Mom had to take anxiety pills and smoke cigarettes because she was an oppressed woman in today's society. Some of this she would tell me outright, and some I would overhear during her coffee time with her friend Peg. They spent many a morning man-bashing both ex-husbands and current husbands.

I did a bit of research and wondered why, if Mom and Peg were such feminists, neither of them had jobs? Why were they both dependent on men for financial support? Larry earned a decent living but was by no means rich. Mom had decided to continue taking classes at the University of Maine but had quit her job at Mixed Doubles as soon as we moved in with Larry and hadn't worked since. She wanted to stay home "with the kids" and have a new baby— then she became a feminist. And in addition to oil painting she had started writing poetry. She frequently read us her poems after dinner as if they were masterpieces. Half the time I didn't understand them but I laid on the compliments because I could tell she really needed them.

I liked to write too but I never wanted anyone to see my stuff. It wasn't pleasant, anyway. Once Mom went searching and found my journal because she wanted to see if I was on drugs. She was disappointed when she found it was written in French and she couldn't understand a word.

One Sunday I was in my room reading when Punky knocked on the door and came in. By that time I had my own room upstairs and she shared a room with Katie in the basement. Katie had moved to her Mom's and just came to visit here and there, much like Mikey, so usually she had the room to herself. "Hey," she said as she sat on the bed. Punky was quiet and kept to herself. It was rare that she came into my room without being invited and I was happy to see her, especially with her having been gone all weekend.

"So...uh... this weekend... when Grandma was in the bathroom, Grandpa took my hand and shoved it in his pants," she blurted out.

You gotta be fucking kidding me, I thought to myself, feeling part of me break off and die.

"Did he make you touch his dick?" Maybe not the most sensitive question to ask a nine-year-old but I quickly went into protector mode. I probably should have hugged her instead but I was the opposite of present and all I could think of was making sure it never happened again.

"I have to tell Mom," I said as I got up from the bed. How could this have happened to sweet little Punky? She was always so pleasant and would never hurt a fly. She didn't deserve to be abused. I had to make it right.

"Mom, Mom, I need to talk to you." I tugged at her sleeve to get her attention. She was painting a landscape and smoking in the kitchen at the breakfast bar. I saw the jug of turpentine and worried for a quick moment that she could blow up the house like the time she lit the couch on fire, but decided Punky's issue was more pressing. "Mom, Arthur made Punky touch his dick."

"What? Oh, come on."

Christ, lady, why would I make this up?

"Mom, it's true. He did it when Lorraine was in the bathroom."

"Send your sister out here," Mom said, still working on her brushstroke.

Mom asked Punky a few questions and concluded she needed to call Frank to let him know his dad was a pedophile. I was so happy she wasn't letting this go. *Maybe she really gets it*, I thought. But I didn't trust her completely. I needed to make sure that sonofabitch never hurt my sister again.

It took a while to reach Frank because he had taken to train hopping which meant he could be anywhere in the country and she had no idea where that anywhere was. He called infrequently, mostly to talk to Punky, but sometimes he'd go for months and Mom thought the situation needed immediate attention. She made a few calls to his best friend in Florida, a man named Flap. I never knew why everyone called him that, but I knew he was a Hell's Angel, super fat, and a buddy from 'Nam.

Within a few days Frank called and Mom told him the news. I eavesdropped on the conversation and Mom cried and then said, "No, Frank, you can't do that!"

When the call was over Mom told us that Frank was coming back to New England to kill his father. I thought it was a brilliant idea and was willing to volunteer my services. I could drive the getaway car, or help dig a hole, though I didn't know how to drive and my digging skills weren't all that great. I'd find a way to help if he needed me. I knew Frank was serious because once Mom left him he felt like he had nothing left to live for, and he spent some time in jail. He used to send me things like hand-stitched leather purses Mom said he made "in the clink." When Mom and Frank were married he used to keep brass knuckles in his nightstand just in case and even though he was sweet to us kids I knew he could do some damage if he was pissed.

I felt vindicated because finally someone was going to pay for hurting a child. Maybe cold-blooded murder was a bit excessive, but truthfully I didn't think so. I was just glad my little sister would get justice and never have to worry about being hurt again. Unfortunately, that feeling was short-lived.

I'm not sure what happened but Frank never showed. He probably drank himself into oblivion after the news had sunk in. That's what I pictured in my head, anyway. Maybe he talked to Lorraine and she cried and talked him out of it. In any event I felt defeated, however at least we could keep little Punky safe from now on.

Less than a few months went by when out of the blue Mom said Arthur and Lorraine were coming to pick up Punky for the weekend.

"What? Are you nuts? She can't go with them!" My heart started racing and my breathing shallowed. The room was closing in.

"She'll be okay," Mom said, dragging hard on her cigarette. She had graduated to Marlborough Lights by now and I was happy that we smoked the same brand. "I'll tell her to stick close to Lorraine."

"Mom, that's not possible! It happened when Lorraine was in the bathroom!"

"Sparrow," Mom said, disgusted with me. "They are buying her summer clothes. They help out a lot. I need them and she's going!" Mom wouldn't look me in the eye because she knew she was a sellout. She knew it and I knew it and she knew that I knew. What happened to the Mom who was angry and wanted to protect her child? How could she pretend what happened was no big deal?

I was split halfway down the middle between terrified and furious. I realized that the weakest link in our family was Mom. It was *Mom* who married those losers, including my kidnapping father. It was *Mom* who couldn't be bothered to cook and clean for us, help us with school, make sure we were presentable. It was *Mom* who kept having children just to ignore them and let them run wild. It was *Mom* who gave our money away to Jim-Fucking-Bakker. It was *Mom* who failed to protect me not once but twice from sick perverts. And now it's *Mom* throwing Punky to the wolves for some cheap Kmart clothes.

I walked away and headed back to my room for a good cry and to strategize. Not for plotting to kill Mom but to ensure little Punky's safety. I was a teenager and even though I lost the dirt ring I was still scrappy. Despite living in the sticks I had become street smart and I was determined to keep my sister safe. At all costs.

Not long after that conversation Mom informed me that Arthur and Lorraine were on the way and would be coming to pick up my sister. She was going to be running errands and left me at the house in charge. I didn't argue but decided to implement my plan. I had spent weeks searching the house to find fool-proof hiding spots. Punky was tiny and could crawl into very tight spaces if need be. I had to find the perfect spot, however, because if someone found her and sent her off with that monster then it would be all my fault. Some things in life are okay to fail at. This was not one of those things.

After much searching I found the spot at the very back of her closet. Her closet was narrow and deep and filled with so much junk that no one ever went in it. There were old broken toys, clothes that didn't even fit Doodie anymore, paper, boxes and trash. From the entrance it looked like Fred Sanford's closet on a bad day and no one would suspect she could make her way back there. I was nervous there were spiders, mice and who knew what else in the closet with no light but we had to take our chances. She could easily live through a spider bite or two.

I had no idea what time they were showing up so I nestled Punky way back in the closet and told her she needed to wait until I came for her. Thank goodness she trusted me and I knew she would do exactly what I said. Once I got her settled in, making sure she could still breathe I went upstairs, locked all the doors and waited. I have no idea exactly how long I waited but it felt like hours. I was sitting on the couch in the family room which looked out over our circular dirt drive so I could see them coming. When I saw the car approaching my heart began pounding like crazy. I crawled onto the carpet and lay flat in front of the couch so they wouldn't see me when they came to the back door.

Within a few minutes the knocking began. I lay perfectly still as they knocked and knocked. My breathing was shallow and adrenaline surged through my body. For a moment I worried that Arthur would kick the door in but then they would only find me. They would have a much harder time finding little Punky.

The knocking went on and on. I felt like I should do something but I couldn't move without someone seeing me. Eventually I heard someone go through the door that led to the three-season porch because there were French doors to the family room there. Thank God I remembered to lock those doors too. I heard the handle jiggle a few times and knew it was Arthur trying his best to get into the house. That man was determined.

When the knocking and jiggling stopped I was still too terrified to move. I hadn't heard the car drive away but then I wondered if I had been too anxious and terrified to notice. I waited as long as I could and when I couldn't take it anymore, I peeked out from the bottom of the couch and there was Arthur, standing at the French doors, looking straight at me. *Oh my God he saw me!* I snapped my head back but it was too late. He knew we were hiding from him. I fully expected the heinous child molester to kick the door in for sure now only he didn't. After a few more minutes I heard the car start and drive away. I finally went to look and they were gone. I still didn't feel we were off the hook so I made Punky stay in hiding until Mom got home.

"What happened? Why is she still here?" Mom asked.

"I told you, she is not going with them. Ever."

Chapter 16

Just like any other girl I was looking forward to turning sixteen. I'm not sure why exactly, except that sixteen felt so much more adult than fifteen. I had a sense that people would take me more seriously and that I would have more privileges. I was also one year closer to freedom. I was ready to celebrate.

The morning of my birthday I was up early getting ready for school. I had decided on a green and white palm-printed shirt and matching wide-leg pants, which were more like culottes since they hit just below the knee. The outfit was rayon so I had let it air dry when I washed it, which meant it had a few wrinkles. I don't think we owned an iron and if we did it was probably at the bottom of Punky's closet, dented, and with a broken cord so I decided to throw my birthday outfit in the dryer for a few minutes to soften out the creases. Our washer and dryer were in the unfinished part of our basement which meant I had to pass Mom's room to get there.

I tiptoed down the stairs, careful to be quiet. We didn't have any rules about not using the dryer in the morning but I still tiptoed because mornings were much nicer when I didn't have to deal with Mom or smell her cigarettes and coffee first thing. After I put the dryer on for ten minutes I tiptoed back up the stairs to finish getting ready. Less than two minutes later I heard someone stomping up the stairs. I figured it was probably Larry and didn't think much of it until I met Mom in the hallway.

"Did you just use the dryer?" she asked, looking and sounding like a wild woman.

"Yes, I was getting some wrinkles out of my outfit."

"You woke me up, Sparrow!" Mom spit-screamed.

"Oh, I'm sorry, Mom. I...I didn't mean to." Even I wasn't on guard at six in the morning.

"How dare you? Your birthday is canceled do you hear me? No cake, no presents, nothing!" I hadn't seen Mom this furious in ages. She was in a total rage meltdown and I'm sure she woke everyone else in the house.

I didn't know what to say so I walked away. I was crushed. My excitement about turning sixteen was gone before it had even set in.

Now it was just another school day.

Mom continued to complain about me out loud as I was in the bathroom finishing my hair, saying things like, "You have no respect!" and "I'm so sick of your shit!" I decided to ignore it because I had spent a great deal of time applying my purple mascara and I didn't want to ruin it with tears. It was still my birthday, after all, and I wanted to look my best.

I was scared to go back downstairs and retrieve my outfit but I took my chances. It couldn't get any worse than canceling my birthday, so what did I have to lose? After I got dressed I hurried out of there as quick as possible, even though I had to stand outside in the November cold to wait for the bus. It was better than the inferno inside my house.

I went through the school day in a bit of a daze. My friends all wished me a happy birthday which I appreciated. I didn't tell anyone what had happened that morning and often didn't spill things like that because I was not one for any kind of sympathy or pity. I did sometimes complain about my crazy parents to my closest friends but I did it in a humorous way and would usually have them all cracking up at the end. Wit and sarcasm were some of my greatest shields.

When I got off the bus that afternoon I had no idea what to expect. I walked in the back door intent on making a bee-line to my bedroom, where I would plop down on my bed and escape with music and my journal, but as I turned the handle and opened the door Mom was there, waiting.

"Happy Birthday, Puppy!" she cried, her eyes sparkling. She threw her arms around me and actually gave me a hug. "Look, here are your presents, and I even got you a lobster!" She pointed to a stack of gifts and a giant steamed lobster staring straight at me from the breakfast bar. There was even cake, too. I was nonplussed.

"Uh...thanks, Mom," was all I could muster as I looked around, wondering why I should trust this moment because it totally felt like a setup. Where were the cameras? I half-expected Larry to pop out of a closet with an ax and start chasing me, but that didn't happen. Even though I should have been happy my body trembled and I wanted to get the hell out of there. Who were these freaks and why was I related to them?

I went to the bathroom to collect myself. Both of my sisters were there and they wanted to celebrate my birthday. I could put on a smile for them and get through this. This wasn't just about me, and if I didn't act thrilled Mom would be mad and call me ungrateful and launch into another one of her crazy spells. I wasn't going to risk that for anything.

Normally I loved presents and cake and lobster but I was too shaken up to enjoy them. Mom must have felt guilty because she had gone to the nice mall and got me some really great clothes, but I just couldn't get excited. I did a good job of pretending, though. It occurred to me that perhaps Mom's medication needed to be adjusted but I was the last person who was going to tell her that, so I just went with it.

After everyone went to bed I poured myself a little shot out of some old bottle of Drambuie I found underneath the kitchen sink, between the dishwasher soap and the Pine Sol. It tasted so bad I think the Pine Sol would have been the better choice but in any event I toasted my sixteenth birthday by myself, in peace.

* * *

Frank didn't make it back for several years after Arthur molested Punky. I'm sure he went on the father of all binges after finding out *his* father was a level-five pedophile. He finally managed to swing a trip shortly after my sixteenth birthday. My birthday part was coincidental but I was happy to see him even though my heart hurt seeing him skinny as a rail and aged beyond his years from alcohol. Seeing him also brought back the memories of all the trips to the VA hospital and the disappointment of our family falling apart. Even though Frank wasn't my father I loved him just as much. He was a good man, and if he had gotten it together we could have still been a family and I wouldn't have been stuck with the step-monster of the century. It was a bittersweet reunion.

Frank camped out on our couch, which was awkward. I was shocked by Larry's graciousness in letting his wife's ex-husband stay at the house. He agreed because he thought it would be good for Punky. On top of that he was nice to Frank, in fact nicer than I had ever seen him. Did the Grinch have a heart after all?

I stayed up later than usual the night Frank got there just to be in his presence. When everyone went to bed, it was just the two of us left talking. I hadn't seen him since I was eleven so it was uncomfortable at first. We talked music a lot. I told him I was into the Grateful Dead and he told me that he had come from the most amazing Pink Floyd concert. He even told me a bit about the joys of train-hopping and how there's a freedom in it.

"I have something for you," Frank said as he got up from the couch and went over to his duffel bag. "Here." He handed me an entire carton of Camel Lights. "Your mom told me you smoke now. Happy Birthday."

"Oh hey, thanks." I took the carton, feeling the oddest mix of gratitude and embarrassment. I was embarrassed for Frank because even though he was no longer my step-dad he *was* and he shouldn't have given me cancer sticks for my birthday. I should have been sneaking them like any good teenager, and he should have been lecturing me on how bad it was for me, like any good parent. I knew he meant well and was trying to connect, but I still felt like no matter where I turned I couldn't escape the freak show.

I gave Frank a hug and inhaled that familiar mix of good ol' Colt 45 and stale cigarette smoke. It didn't make me love him any less. After all those years I was certain he still loved me and I was certain he would always smell like that.

* * *

The beginning of junior year was exciting for a few reasons. I no longer felt invisible at school. I was officially an upperclassman, well, upperclasswoman, though I wore lots of ties and oxford shirts because that's what girls were wearing in *Cosmo* and *Seventeen*. Even though I lived in the sticks I was determined not to look the part. I still had a pair of steel-toed shitkickers Larry bought me one Christmas so I could make my way to the shed and bring in firewood in the snow. I never wore them in public, however, even though lots of other girls at school did. One girl had her yearbook picture taken in a plaid flannel shirt and holding a rather large piglet. On top of that she had a terrible feathered haircut and giant, round glasses that engulfed her cute face. I desperately wanted to give her a makeover but she was less than interested. For a brief moment I wondered what it would be like to be that frumpy. Perhaps uncles and step-dads and pediatricians and random drunk boys at parties would leave you alone? Maybe they wouldn't notice you at all. I dismissed the thought, knowing I was too boy crazy to go to school with so much as a chipped nail. I was already a goner.

The other reason I was happy in eleventh grade was because one of my other big crushes, Chase Robertson, had returned to school. He was a blond-haired, blue-eyed boy two years ahead of me who had disappeared in my freshman year; rumor had it he had gone to juvie. I had only talked with him a few times but for some reason had developed an intense crush. It could have been how he combed his hair numerous times a day at school. It could have been his perfect smile, though he really didn't smile often. Let's face it, it was probably the brand new white Pontiac Firebird he was driving, a gift from his parents. In reality he wasn't all that cute, and his face was so greasy Jess used to joke that she could fry an egg on it. Nevertheless, I was smitten.

Chase was the only boy at school with his own apartment, which was fun to go to after school because in exchange for doing Egg Face's homework I got to smoke cigarettes and enjoy a few shots of vodka. Even though my grades mostly sucked it was merely lack of effort, not a lack of brain cells. I could whip out an essay on almost anything and he was in some lower-level classes so it wasn't tough. I used to lie and tell Mom I was getting extra help after school. She didn't have a clue and as long as I was home early enough to do dishes or bring in wood it was alright on occasion.

On one of those random days Egg Face and I had our usual make-out session on his couch but this time he stood up, grabbed my hand and led me to his bedroom. I was still a virgin, not for lack of trying. I had tried to have sex with a guy named Jake I had dated the summer before but we didn't know he should have purchased the lubricated Trojans and there wasn't even a chance of it happening so we played video games instead. My guess was that Egg Face knew what he was doing and I was right. He expertly lowered me onto his twin bed and unbuttoned my pink-and-white floral shirt, tossing it onto the floor. Next, he managed to slide my jeans off, one leg and then the other. I kind of faded out a little after that, fearing that staying in my body wasn't the best idea since I didn't know what to expect.

I came back to the room the moment he entered me. *Fuck, this hurts*, was all I could think. I opened my eyes to scan the room, looking for something to fixate on in hopes of being able to manage the pain. That wasn't a great idea, because there on his dresser to the left of the bed was an 8x10 picture of Egg Face and his ex-girlfriend, Andrea. My heart froze, and I had two choices: be devastated and cry because I was losing my virginity to a guy still in love with his ex, or go numb and just finish what I started. I chose the latter, though he was the only one who actually finished. Not that I knew much about finishing. I don't recall a single conversation about the birds and the bees but I had read *The Joy of Sex* and the smut Grandma had lent me. I kind of knew what an orgasm was intellectually, I had just never had one. Mom had taken Grandma's book from me before I could finish and though I still learned a few things it wasn't really educational smut.

After our six minutes of heaven Egg Face and I got up and put our clothes back on. I took one more shot of vodka for the road and we headed to my house. Egg Face never came inside and wanted nothing to do with meeting my family. We drove in silence until he pulled into my driveway and I said goodbye as I kissed his cheek. What was I supposed to do? I had no idea what was customary for such an occasion. Should I tell him thanks for making my vagina feel like it had shards of glass sticking out of it? Or perhaps I should high five him and say, "Well done, you!" I couldn't think straight because I just wanted to tear off my soggy panties and race to the shower. I could still smell latex and I decided it was a smell I could do without, especially between my legs.

I forgot to mention God has cursed me with a heightened sense of smell. It was one of the reasons I was such a picky eater. If food was pungent I often couldn't handle it. Total sensory overload, even if it tasted okay. Case in point: mayonnaise. From the time I was a tiny girl I couldn't stand the smell of any kind of mayo. Some people say Miracle Whip is not mayonnaise but they are full of shit; it smells the same to me. There's no logical reason I should be averse to the stuff as I love eggs and I'm fine with oil, so why does the smell of mayonnaise disgust me? I could smell it on someone's sandwich a half mile away and I'd start dry-heaving instantly. Mom never bought it or used it so I was safe at home but when I went to Dad's and was faced with macaroni salad I was screwed.

Thank God we used protection, I thought as I scrubbed my bits gently in the shower, though it felt like I was using one of those Brillo pads Mom made me use to scrub the pots that sometimes sat for a few days. I was on fire. I knew the pain would go away, I was just thankful that we were careful and I didn't have to freak out about having some poor greasy-faced baby who would be teased by all the other babies at daycare for looking like I rubbed Alberto V05 on his poor little mug. I was pretty sure I was supposed to be feeling warm fuzzies, or butterflies, or something lovely but instead I felt dirty. Used. I had just lost something I could never get back. The worst part was he didn't deserve it. Not if he wasn't madly in love with me. I couldn't get that picture of Egg Face and Andrea out of my head. She had dumped his ass and I was the runner-up. The consolation prize. *Way to go, Sparrow.*

Going to school the next day was awkward. I wondered if I looked different to anyone, or walked differently. Could people tell I'd had sex last night? Could they smell the latex? I decided not to tell anyone, not even my girlfriends. I wanted to sit on this for a bit, perhaps even pretend it never happened.

Later that day in algebra my friend JD was making conversation and asked what I did the night before. "Oh, nothing much." Egg Face was also in the same class and was sitting a few seats back so he'd overheard the conversation. It must have upset him because right after school he dumped me.

"Things are over between us," he said when I went up to his car after class.

"What? What are you talking about?"

"I heard your conversation with JD in class. You told him you did nothing last night. Didn't it mean anything to you?"

"Of course it did," said, flustered. "I wasn't going to tell him, though."

"Well, clearly you don't care about me, so we're through." Egg Face huffed as he got into his car and sped away. I stood there, devastated. If I felt used last night I felt completely discarded now. What was worse was that I saw through his bullshit. I knew he was just looking for an excuse to leave me since he had gotten what he wanted. How could I have not seen this coming? Normally I was so good at holding my feelings in but not this time. I cried like a child, heaving sobs from my core. It was the fallout of every man in my life who had neglected me, used me and abused me all in one.

It didn't take long before a few friends saw me melting and came over to help.

"What happened?" They asked. I let it all out as I cried and cried, which was so unlike me. I had no defenses.

"That son of a bitch!" Joey said. "I'll kick his ass, Sparrow!"

"No, Joey, don't get crazy, please!"

Joey was a good friend of mine. He was also in my algebra class and sat right in front of me, usually sleeping with his head down on the desk. He had black hair, blue eyes, and wore the same black leather motorcycle jacket every day. He never said much except, "Got a smoke?" I'm pretty sure he slept like that in every class so I have no idea how he passed anything. "Get in my car," he said, motioning over to where he was parked. "I'll take you home."

I cried and smoked as Joey drove to the next town where I lived. He was sweet when we got there as he opened my car door and walked me up the stairs to the back door.

"Don't worry, Sparrow, everything will be okay," he whispered as he hugged me. I settled my head into his neck and exhaled. It felt nice to have a friend to lean on, especially one who was strong and more than a little tough. Anyone with a wallet on a chain could kick greasy Egg Face's ass, not that I wanted that. But I felt safe. Protected.

"Thanks, J," I muttered as I pulled away to go into my house. Before I could fully break our embrace he grabbed my face with both hands and kissed me. Well, tried. I pulled back instantly.

"What are you doing?"

Is he nuts? I'm crying over another guy!

"Sparrow, that guy didn't deserve you. I'll treat you like a princess," he said as he leaned in to suck my face again.

"Dude, get the fuck off me!" I yelled, pissed. What the hell was he thinking? I thought he was being a friend! Turns out he was looking for his opportunity. I punched him in the arm a few times then turned on my heels and slammed the door behind me. What an asshole. My whole pity party lasted an entire ten minutes before I had to go from victim back to survivor again. For once I wanted to be able to let my guard down, but that was not to be my fate.

Word got around fast at school that Egg Face had taken my innocence and broken my heart. I couldn't believe what happened next. People came out of the woodwork to support me. The following day in algebra when Egg Face left to use the bathroom a girl I barely knew grabbed his books off the desk and hurled them out the window. I hadn't said a word to her. She looked over at me and smiled before she went back to her seat. After school some guy friends of mine roughed Egg Face up as he was getting in his car.

They didn't kick his ass entirely, but they pushed him around a little, and one keyed his car on the driver's side.

Egg Face thought I was out for revenge. When I heard the stories it did feel vindicating, but I had no hand in any of it. I was shocked, however, that people were supporting me. I couldn't recall when that had ever happened. I certainly didn't think I was important enough for people to risk getting into trouble. Even as a junior I wasn't overly confident and thought people were just nice to my face. I didn't realize so many people cared, especially about my deflowering.

My enjoyment of the attention came to a major halt that night when Egg Face called.

"What do you want?" I asked purposely sounding annoyed. What could this wanker possibly want from me?

"You had better tell your friends to leave me alone, or I'm going to kill you."

"I had nothing to do with any of that, Chase."

"Bullshit. You're such a bitch. If it doesn't stop I'm going to cut you into tiny pieces, Sparrow, and no one will ever find you." I felt the blood drain from my face. By then I had a good sixth sense for danger and I could tell he was serious. After all, he did go to juvie for a long time, and I never knew what for. I assumed it was for stealing car stereos because once when we went to the local fair a screwdriver fell out of his coat and I had noticed he was looking in car windows as we were coming out of the parking lot. Egg Face was a loner. He was dark, serious and didn't talk much. When he did talk he was insulting someone. I wouldn't put it past him to chop me up with a chainsaw. At least that was what I was picturing in my head. Larry happened to walk by and I handed him the phone.

"Chase is threatening to kill me," I whispered as I gave over the cordless. I'm not sure what made me get Larry involved since he never once supported or defended me in any way. Maybe I wanted to see what would happen with two giant egos on the phone. Or maybe I was just plain scared and hoped he'd come to my defense.

"Chase, what's this I hear about you threatening Sparrow?" There was a long silence as he listened. His face got redder and I saw my favorite vein bulging in his forehead. "Now listen here you little..." He didn't get to finish because Egg Face had hung up, but not before threatening to cut Larry into tiny pieces too. This was serious. "That kid's the devil! You're no longer allowed to hang out with him!" Of course he was clueless, as usual. I know I'd made some poor choices from time to time but even on my worst day I wouldn't spend time with someone who threatened to murder me. But I guess in his way Larry was trying to protect me. Or himself, for that matter. In any event I wasn't messing around.

That night I got the cot out and set it up in Mom and Larry's room. This was a new low. Never have I been so scared that I needed to sleep with my parents. Even when I was little I didn't have the type of parents that were warm and fuzzy and you wanted to crawl in bed with. This was different. My life was at stake and I wasn't taking any chances. For one whole week I slept in their room, listening to Larry saw some serious logs, knowing that less than a foot away in Larry's sock drawer there was a hollow, pink, rubber dildo underneath his tube socks. Once I had looked for a pair of socks to borrow and there it was. It looked like a glossy pink earthworm. I thought for sure it belonged to Mom but I got pissed at her one time and tried to throw it in her face.

"Whatever, Mom, I found your pink dildo," I said trying to shut her up. I thought she would be furious but instead she giggled.

"Actually, that belongs to your step-dad. He likes a little backdoor fun." Mom never missed an opportunity to throw Larry under the bus, but I could tell she was telling the truth. Way too much truth, as usual.

That week I spent on the cot was easily one of the worst weeks of my teenage years. But I was lucky because once Egg Face and I had broken up, he left school. I guess he realized he didn't have many friends, and on top of that he was harassed by mine. He didn't even last a week, which was why I was finally able to sleep in my own bed. It was rumored he went back to Florida.

A few months later I took my own trip to Florida with Jess, her mom and her brother Robbie. They were going to Miami for spring break and invited me along. I was thrilled to be included. Going to a beach was my favorite thing to do even though I was scared of sharks and jellyfish. I'd still get in the water, but I was always on the lookout. Luckily I never encountered either. I was surprised Mom let me go, but in truth she was more and more out of it because of all the meds she was taking.

Another reason Mom didn't object to my spring break trip was because she didn't have to pay for it. The O' Tooles took me on several trips and always insisted on paying my way. I also had spending money from working. Mom and Larry had tried confiscating my very first paycheck, saying that since I was working I should pay rent. I told them they were ridiculous and to go fuck themselves. Mom chased me around the house trying to snatch my check out of my hand, but I stuck it in my bra and told her I'd fight her if she came near me. Part of me wanted her to come at me. I was sixteen and a whole two inches taller than her. Sure she was a lot larger than me but I had figured out how I could take her to the ground. First I would grab her arm and twist it behind her back. Next I would knee her in the back and push her to the ground face-first. I hadn't quite figured out what I would do after that. Probably just sit on her until she apologized for being such a shitty mom. Part of me is glad it never went that far.

Going on vacation with the O' Tooles was a blast. Jess's mom was cool and let us do what we wanted. The condo we stayed in was right on the water. It had two floors with an elevator. We stayed upstairs in one room and Jess's brother Robbie was in the other. Jess's mom stayed downstairs, so we had our privacy. There was an intercom system so she could buzz us if she needed us to come down.

Our first night there Jess and I decided to take a walk down the strip to see if we could meet anyone our age or older. It didn't take but five minutes before this super-hot guy pulled up in a burgundy Corvette Stingray.

"Hey, you girls wanna go to a party?" Jess and I looked at each other.

"Yeah, sure!" she said. Jess hopped in first and we both squished into the front seat.

"Hi, I'm Alejandro, but you can call me Alex. What are your names?"

We told him, along with where we were from and that we were spring breakers. Alex was twenty and worked in construction. He was half Cuban and spoke both English and Spanish fluently. He had light brown hair, blues eyes and a darker complexion. His teeth were straight and brilliantly white and he had a perfect physique—muscular but not overly so. His body screamed triathlete.

We showed up at the party but it was lame and we didn't stay long. Alex introduced Jess to his friend Jon because Alex was interested in me. He couldn't take his eyes off me and he was sporting the cutest and goofiest grin I'd seen in a long time. We ended up going back to his apartment to hang out and have some drinks. Alex had a great stereo so we jammed out to some music and got high. A song started playing and Alex sang the lyrics to me, something about how he was going to house me and that I was in his hut.

It was sexy but I was already smitten. Not long after he picked me up and carried me to his bedroom. Jess and Jon were making out on the couch so I didn't feel guilty leaving her.

Alex's room was nice for a twenty-year-old bachelor. It was tidy and his bed was made. He had another great stereo in his room and he put on some more mellow music. Even though he was amazing and my hormones were raging and I was tipsy and high I decided I wouldn't have sex with him. I didn't want him to think I was sleazy and I actually liked him, so I didn't want to screw it up. We made out for what seemed like forever and our shirts came off, but that was it. I wasn't going to give it away again so easily. He didn't pressure me at all and was a complete gentleman. I even fell asleep for a little bit and when I woke up he was staring at me and playing with my hair.

"I'm sorry I fell asleep," I muttered, a little embarrassed.

"It's okay, I really enjoy looking at you. You are *so* beautiful. Where did you come from?"

I laughed it off because I was not used to compliments and attention like that. It seemed sweet and genuine and it made me uncomfortable, but I still forced myself to enjoy the moment.

I could have stayed there like that for days, but we had to go back to the condo. Alex dropped us off, giving me a hug and kiss before he left.

"I'll call you tomorrow. I'd like to see you as much as possible while you're here."

I was thrilled to hear that and while I'd normally play it cool, I decided not to torture him because he didn't deserve it.

"We're hitting the beach tomorrow, so come say hi." I'd gotten a killer new bathing suit and I wanted him to see me in it. It was a neon pink and yellow one piece that looked like a bikini in the front but was connected on the sides.

I was on cloud nine when we tiptoed back into the condo, careful not to wake anyone. Jess and I crawled into bed, giggling.

"So," she whispered, "How was he?"

"Jess! I didn't sleep with him. We just made out. I really like him, though."

"Oh," Jess said, her voice flat. "Well, I slept with Jon."

"Jessica! Are you kidding? Why? You just met him!"

"I know, but he's cute and we're on vacation. No one will know."

Jess had no restraint when it came to anything. Food, alcohol, drugs, boys. She was the queen of excess. I was pissed because I knew what this meant. Jon had gotten what he wanted so he wasn't going to call her. And if she didn't have a boy to hang out with then I wouldn't be able to hang out with Alex, which would completely crush my soul. *I hope I'm wrong*, I thought, as I drifted off to sleep with visions of Alex and me in his hot car, holding hands while listening to house music and planning our happily ever after.

Alex made good on his word and tried to see me as much as he could the whole time I was there. I was right about Jon; he had fallen off the face of the Earth. I finally got up the nerve to ask Alex.

"So, how come Jon hasn't called Jess?"

"Well, he really isn't into your friend." Alex said, looking away.

"Do you have any other friends we could fix her up with?" I didn't want to miss out on anything, especially because Jess couldn't keep her panties on.

"Not really. I'll think on it, though," Alex said. We were definitely on the same page. We enjoyed each other's company so much and we needed to make this work.

Alex never did find another friend but we somehow got to spend time together. I talked with Jess's mom and asked if I could spend one whole day with Alex and she said yes. Jess wasn't thrilled about it but she said she understood. I didn't feel guilty, especially when I thought of her betrayal regarding Phil. I decided she could suck it up.

On our day together Alex took me to the Miami zoo and the Everglades. I was blown away by both. We walked and talked and melted together in the heat. There were lots of exotic birds at the zoo and the Everglades was spectacular. We were sitting on a bank with alligators just ten feet away. I was terrified at first and thought I needed to add gators to my list of water fears, but Alex insisted we were fine. He even threw tiny rocks at their noses which were barely sticking up out of the water. I'm not sure what he would have done if a gator had come out of the water after us, but I still felt safe with him.

That night Alex took me to meet his mother. I was a surprised and a little nervous, but it seemed important to him so I agreed. Nereida (Nettie for short) was a beautiful woman in her late forties. She had short dark hair, dark eyes and a warm smile. Walking into her bungalow was like stepping into a novelty shop. Her entire house was decorated in Betty Boop. Everything was red, white and black. White sofas, red rugs, black lacquer furniture, and pictures of Betty everywhere you turned. There were Betty Boop statues and clocks—literally everything was homage to Miss Boop and her little dog whose name escapes me. Nettie was a good hostess and asked me all about my life. She had an exotic accent and you could tell she really loved her son. Nettie was single and lived alone but she didn't seem to mind. I don't know if any man would have been able to live in a Betty Boop museum and I'm sure it didn't faze her. She seemed like a woman totally at ease with herself.

Meeting Alex's mom deepened the connection between Alex and me. That night back at his apartment I decided to go all the way with him. If I didn't I thought I might always regret it. And after the whole Egg Face incident I needed a do-over.

I pretended being with Alex was my first time. I was totally present and nothing about Alex and the experience made me want to leave my body. He was gentle and really took his time. I had messed around with boys before but this was different—Alex felt like a man to me. Grown up, mature, with his own apartment and even a Corvette. Who cared if it kept overheating?

Alex spent lots of time looking into my eyes and brushing the hair back from my face. He played his Guns N' Roses CD and put the song "Patience" on repeat. I lost my virginity for the second time to one of the best songs of all time with the best guy I had ever met. Could this get any better? Maybe even God thought I needed to be plucked properly. How else can I explain the perfection of that moment?

After that evening I wanted to be naked with Alex every day until I had to leave. He seemed fine with that and so began my Intro to Sex 101. I learned how to be on top, how to flex my Kegels, how to master the art of oral pleasure, and on and on. He was an amazing teacher and I was an eager learner. He gave wonderful compliments and feedback that boosted my confidence tremendously. We even showered together which was daunting at first but very intimate. I decided I liked it and I didn't care if my hair got wet or my makeup ran down my face. I was in love.

On our last night together my heart weighed a thousand pounds. I couldn't believe I had met the most amazing guy and I had to leave him. He was equally bereft. Our minds raced as we tried to figure out how we could keep what we had going. Could he fly to Maine? Could I come back? We could talk on the phone each week, write letters, send carrier pigeons.

"I don't want to lose you," he said, tearing up a little.

We hugged and I could feel how much he cared about me. The only other person who had ever hugged me like that was Grandpa Johnny. This was more intense. This was raw.

When we were finally able to tear ourselves away from each other Alex reluctantly got into his car and I watched him drive off. My heart was heavy, like cement. I swallowed my tears because I didn't want to be a downer for Jess. I'm sure she was disappointed that I had spent so much time with Alex. "Let's walk down to the beach," I said as I went over to her and grabbed her arm. I had gotten some pot from Alex who was an occasional smoker and I wanted to get high and numb out. We copped a squat close to the water, smoked the whole blunt and got high as hell. I was relieved to have made most of the pain go away. I went from feeling like crawling under a rock to almost laughing. Luckily it was late and the beach was empty because I'm sure people could tell we were high from a mile away.

We made our way back to the condo because Jess was hungry. We tried hard to act normal but we were both still crazy high and Jess had started hallucinating. "Sparrow, look, my arms are floating away!" she shrieked, sounding alarmed yet laughing at the same time.

I couldn't see her arms floating but I did see her face grow and shrink a few times. *I hate it when I smoke too much*, I thought. But once you are high there is nothing you can do except wait for the stuff to wear off. The only other time I had gotten this high was at a Great White concert with Gwen. She smoked all the time and had this incredible tolerance. I tried to keep up with her which was a terrible mistake. There I was, standing in the crowd at the show when I blacked out, which is bad enough, however I was still conscious and awake (although extremely high) yet I couldn't see. I was completely blind.

"Gwen! I can't see!"

"Get on someone's shoulders!"

"No, Gwen, I'm blind! I can't see!" I'd been through a lot in my short life but I had never lost my vision. I was trying not to panic but it was getting scary. Gwen didn't miss a beat. She grabbed my arm and dragged me off the floor and over to the side where there were seats.

"Sit here and relax. You'll be okay." She rubbed my head and hugged me. She was the best. And she was right. In about ten minutes my vision returned and we were able to enjoy the rest of the concert. I had never been so relieved. We even got back on the floor. I was still high and completely paranoid; I was sure someone's lighter was going to set my hair on fire. That was big hair era and my giant, crunchy hair was probably highly flammable.

One would think I would have learned my lesson and steered clear of any more marijuana but far from it. I was careful not to smoke too much for the most part, but tonight was an exception. I didn't care if I lost my eyesight again because I couldn't see Alex's sweet face anymore. What was the point of having eyes?

When we got back to our room Jess found a bag of chips and we dove in.

"Girls, I need you to come down here, please," said a voice over the intercom.

"Oh no! Who was that?" I said.

"Did you hear that? Oh my God it's my mother!" Jess said as she choked on her chip. She jumped up and went over to the intercom.

"Mom, we're busy, what do you need?"

"I just want to check in with you and go over details for tomorrow," Mrs. O'Toole said, annoyed. Jess was able to think on her feet and I realized she had probably been in this type of situation before. I was paralyzed with fear.

"Mom, Sparrow's sick and I'm helping her. We can't come down now. We'll see you in the morning." Wow, great save. Will she buy it?

"Are you ok, honey?" Mrs. O. asked me.

"Yes, I just have a stomach ache." I didn't like lying, but there was nothing else I could do.

"Well, get some rest. See you in the morning."

Off the hook. Thank God! We giggled over that one for what seemed like an hour before we passed out.

Alex and I kept in touch as much as we could after I returned home. My heart ached for him and it was like having a ton of weight on my chest. I never cried but I was depressed. We tried to call each other weekly but we had to be careful because it was expensive to make long distance calls back then and Larry was pissed each month when the phone bill came. After several months our calls gradually decreased until it was mostly Alex making them, and just on major holidays. We never saw each other again.

Chapter 17

That summer Jess and I were bored and since she was always
looking for a thrill it was never hard to find one. She had been
getting into some heavier drugs and I wasn't at all interested. She
had the luxury of killing brain cells since her parents were rich and
would probably leave her millions. My family wasn't leaving me shit
and so I knew I would have to make my own way in the world.
There was no way I was going to string myself out on LSD or
cocaine. A few kids at school talked about some fancy drug called
"crystal" that they had tried on the West coast but I wasn't
interested in that either. I was good with the occasional blunt,
rolled in my favorite hot pink, leopard print rolling papers because
even then I was a bit of a diva.

Jess used to drive her mother's dark blue Audi but she crashed
it, so for a while she drove a brown van with stripes we called the
PV (party van). It was fun because we could fit a ton of people in it
and Jess would drive, totally fucked up, as we partied in the back.
Needless to say she crashed that car too by hitting a giant buck in
the middle of the road at 2am. Her parents learned their lesson and
bought her an old, green Ford LTD that was a total tank. We
nicknamed it Lurch. There was no wrecking that thing.
Surprisingly Jess wasn't at all embarrassed to drive it, even though
it was a beater and the interior was worn to shreds. It just meant it
was no big deal if someone spilled beer or puked inside it.

Jess would pick me up in Lurch and we'd drive to Portland where the real mall was. It was a good hour away but the clothes were more stylish and sometimes it was just nice to get out of the sticks. The clothes were more expensive but it didn't matter because we stole them all anyway. I hated stealing because it made my adrenaline soar but I loved having cool new clothes so I decided it was worth it. We had started stealing small things like makeup and stuffed animals, but then Jess showed me how to take more expensive things like Guess jeans and fancy dresses. It was easy. All you had to do was take items into the dressing room to try on, remove the tags, and then put the clothes on underneath the baggy clothes you wore to the store. We stood up on the bench, lifted up a suspended ceiling tile and shoved the tags and hangers up there. This way there was no evidence. We typically hit the big department stores and usually there was no one around to check us into the dressing rooms. Most days there weren't sales people on the floor at all. It was effortless.

Jess decided it was better for us to rent a locker in the mall so we could take more so we would bring bags, go to the bathroom to unload, then put the bags in the locker before we hit the next store. At the end of the day we would add up how much we had stolen (retail value) based on memory and see who was able to pilfer the most. My record day was five hundred dollars. I was ecstatic with only a twinge of guilt. I rationalized it because my parents hardly ever bought me clothes and I felt too good to be walking around in rags just because they were miserly.

I had a reputation of having good taste in clothes at school and I needed to keep it up. It all started in eighth grade. I had begged Mom to let me pick out my own school clothes after the seventh grade fiasco when she did it for me. She gave me one hundred fifty dollars and told me that was all I was getting. I scoured the mall all day and found the best deals for the coolest items and that whole year my classmates raved about my clothes. I finally felt like I was significant in some way and there was no way I was giving that up. In fact, I took it to the next level which is when I began stealing.

I may have been a thief but I had a harder time being a liar. Before long Mom noticed my outfits, as I'm sure I looked like I'd stepped out of *Seventeen* magazine.

"Where are you getting all these nice clothes?" she asked one day.

I was wearing a blue-knit top that hung off the shoulder and expensive faded-denim shorts. I was surprised by her question because Mom never noticed much about me. She wasn't the kind of mom who would ask to see my report card, (which wasn't great those days), and she never noticed when I did something different with my hair. Why was she noticing my new clothes?

"I stole them. Because you don't buy me anything," I added. Not only did Mom or Larry hate spending money on me, they also had forced me to quit my part-time job at the umbrella store because they refused to drive me when there were times I was scheduled without my friends and no one was available to take me.

I hated having no money, but there was no place close to get a job. There was one store at the end of my street called Wally's. Wally's General Store, to be exact. It was a small, metal building with chipped blue paint. Inside, which was incredibly dusty and old, there were jars of pickled pig's feet on the shelves that dated back to the sixties and cans of green beans that were pre-WWII. I had no idea how the place even stayed in business, except that it was the only store around for miles. I think they did most of their business in gasoline and beer, and the junk food that my friends and I purchased. My favorite things to get at Wally's were the Fortune Bubble bubble gum which had a fortune in every piece and the dill pickle potato chips. Mikey's favorites were Bomb Pops and ketchup chips, no doubt a reminder of his earlier years of gorging on ketchup sandwiches. I would have died before working there.

"Well, please stop stealing, Sparrow," Mom said. I could tell she was taken aback a bit by my honesty. And let's face it; I was probably trying to make her feel bad, suggesting she was reducing me to thievery because she wouldn't spend money on me. I was surprised she didn't yell or try to lecture me. Normally Mom would throw out some Bible quote and tell you what Jesus thought of stealing, but this time it was surprisingly dropped and I counted my blessings.

Several months later Mom was mad at me for talking back and arguing with her because I wanted to go to a friend's house. She must have been in the throes of PMS because she got a crazed look on her face and said, "I'm turning you in for stealing." Mom knew how to twist the knife if you rubbed her the wrong way. I'm sure I started it with my smart-ass comments but she caught me off guard. These two incidents were totally unrelated but Mom wanted to win this one.

"You don't even know where I got the stuff."

"Well, I know you must have gotten the Guess jeans from Porteous. I'm calling them." Porteous (pronounced Porch-iss) was one of the stores I stole from on a regular basis. Mom went to find the cordless phone. *I wonder if she is bluffing. Shit, what if she really turns me in? Would she do that to her own daughter?* I waited to see if she would follow through and to my surprise she sure did.

Driving up to Porteous was worse than uncomfortable, but I wasn't going to let it show. *These people can't break me,* I kept thinking to myself. Mom had filled Larry in on my new hobby and he was more than happy to drive me an hour one way to turn my "prima donna" ass in. To show any shame or remorse would have been admitting defeat, and that wasn't going to happen.

When we got to the store Mom asked for the manager. I can't remember his name but she had spoken to him on the phone and he was expecting us. I had two articles of clothing with me: the denim shorts and that cute knit top that hung off the shoulder.

Mom had no clue about how many things I had taken and I couldn't remember what came from which store so we settled on those two items.

I was surprised when the manager came out. He was in his early thirties, tall, well built, and dreamy. He had kind eyes and a disarming smile as he introduced himself to us. Punky and Doodie were with us too, and we all followed him into his posh office. It looked like something out of *Horse & Hound* with the dark wood, built-in bookcases and forest green wing-back chairs

"Have a seat, everyone," dreamy manager said. When we were all seated, Dreamboat turned to look at me. Any walls I had up were melted by his warm, blue eyes.

"So, young lady, I hear you've been stealing from my store. Is that correct?" How did he make accusing me of theft sound so warm? I was expecting a stern lecture and lots of threats. I was prepared for it. I had planned on sitting stone-faced and not saying a word. Instead Dreamboat found my wall's kill switch and I started talking.

"I'm really sorry for stealing. My parents made me quit my job and I haven't had any money lately."

"Oh, that's a bummer," he said. "Where were you working?"

"I was working in an umbrella store. It was okay but not that exciting. They were paying me four-fifty an hour though, better than minimum wage." We were actually having a dialog. I was able to have a meaningful conversation with an authority figure, which I could not remember having in eons.

"I'm sorry you're no longer working, but how come you didn't ask your parents to buy these clothes for you?" For a moment I had forgotten there was anyone else in the room. I was looking at Dreamboat and he was looking at me. Not through me, *at* me. And he was interested in my life.

"Well, my step-dad always reminds me that I'm not his kid and he doesn't want to pay for things for me. He tells me to ask my real dad, but he lives far away and only sends money on my birthday. Plus, I feel bad begging. He sometimes has money problems." Dreamboat's eyes softened. He could tell I was telling the truth. I wasn't meaning to throw my family under the bus, but maybe I was. It didn't matter though because I was telling the God's honest truth. That was my reality.

"I'll tell you what," Dreamboat started. "I'm not going to call the police or press charges. Normally I would, but if you promise me you will never steal again I will forget this ever happened. Can you promise me?"

Are you kidding? I would promise you my firstborn right now.

"Yes, sir, I promise I will never steal again." I was relieved and also proud of myself for not crying. I smiled. It was a moment to capture.

"Of course, I'll need your parents to pay for these clothes. Without tags I can't take them back so you should keep them." Mom and Larry were stunned. Dreamboat motioned for us to follow him and then led my parents to the counter so they could pay for my outfit. Eighty-six dollars later and a hug from Dreamboat and we were on our way. Best trip to the mall. Ever.

Driving home the ride was silent up front. I was giddy and playing with Doodie, singing her songs and telling her stories. I was delighted that Larry's big plan to shame me backfired. What an epic fail. Maybe that was his bad karma for killing a piece of my soul in that New York mall a few years back? I was relishing the fact that they couldn't break me. I was a bad ass.

"You know, I'm sick of your cavalier attitude!" Larry yelled, startling everyone. "You have no remorse! It's my job to teach you a lesson! We're going to Wally's and you're confessing to stealing those wine coolers!" Larry had the rage thing going again. His face was beet red and he was banging his fist on the steering wheel. He must have been stewing the entire ride because we were just a mile away from Wally's which was less than half a mile from our house.

To back up two years prior my friend Jamie had stolen a bunch of wine coolers from Wally's while I was the lookout. We drank them in a tent we pitched in her barn but she was naive enough to save the bottle caps and her mom found them later. Jamie was so drunk she pissed in our tent. I only drank a few and even though I was buzzed pretty good I wasn't tanked like her and I never would have pissed on anything for obvious reasons. We ended up having to sneak into her house to sleep since everything was soaked.

The next day I was hung over yet still rode my bike to Dana's house. Mom pulled up shortly after in the car, honking for me to come out. When I did she was shaking a cup full of bottle caps. "You're grounded. Get in the car!"

I remained calm.

"First off, I didn't do any stealing, and second that was two years ago and I already served my time for that." How could he be so unreasonable? I knew he just wanted to break me.

"I don't care! You're gonna go in and apologize to Wally himself!"

Wally was a hefty older man. He looked Greek with his dark wavy hair and olive complexion. He wore a dirty, white apron over his giant belly and always had a lit cigar in his mouth. Wally had a little butcher shop in the back of the store and his apron always had some kind of blood and guts smeared on it. Who knows? Maybe he was chopping up kids who had stolen from him. I wasn't about to find out.

As Larry approached the four-way stop where Wally's was I saw my opportunity and took it. As the car slowed down I opened the left side passenger door and dove out. He wasn't going fast, maybe ten miles an hour, but it still scraped me up some. I was careful to make sure I had my stolen-yet-recently-purchased outfit in hand. I know I rolled once, I may have rolled twice, but at least it was in the direction of home.

As soon as I could stand I gathered myself and booked it toward the house. Mom saw what I did first so she screamed her typical Mom scream, like someone was being murdered by clowns. Larry slammed on the brakes and Mom hit her head on the windshield, ranting about whiplash. Doodie was crying in the back, Larry was screaming and of course Punky was silent, as usual, taking it all in. I wanted nothing to do with this freak show family.

Once again, I won. I beat them home, probably because Mom made Larry go to Wally's for more cigarettes. I holed up in my room with my heavy dresser barricading the door and I put my stereo on, smoked cigarettes and celebrated my success. No one bothered to pound on my door this time, which was refreshing. And, I kept my promise to Dreamboat and never stole anything ever again.

Chapter 18

The rest of junior year was uneventful. I was asked to prom by a quiet guy named Roland Tweed. He was average height, slightly lanky and had wavy, coarse dark hair—a total Jew fro. I actually don't know if he was Jewish or not and it wouldn't have mattered, except for some reason East Coast people tend to be obsessed about nationality. If your last name wasn't Hispanic or Italian everyone wondered if you were a Jew. It reminded me of how some people are really into cars. Going down the road with Dad and Mikey was always a lesson in cars for me. I can still identify cars better than any female I know, not that I want to or really care, it's just an ingrained habit now and maybe it's my way of remaining close to them.

I didn't know Roland well but Dana convinced me to go with him so we could double-date with her and her boyfriend Dave. Larry was working and Mom loved spending his money when he wasn't around to bitch so she piled the kids in the car and took me to the nice mall. I got a gorgeous dark blue taffeta dress that looked black when you moved the fabric a certain way. It was strapless and above the knee and it fit just like a glove. I couldn't wait to wear it.

The prom was on a Friday night. Dana dropped me off at home after school so I could get ready, then she was coming back to pick me up. I worried about riding up front since her super-old Cutlass had a giant hole in the front passenger floorboard and I didn't want anything to happen to my dress or shoes. Normally we put a bunch of cardboard down and I would hold it in place with my feet but once it fell out and I could see the road right below me as she was driving. This time I would sit in the back.

When I got home that day no one else was there. Larry was off ruining the environment with his pesticides and Mom and the kids were shopping. I saw the answering machine light blinking so I pushed the button.

"Hello, this is Howard Sterling, the Dean here at Barrington Academy. Sparrow, I know you're planning a party after prom and I just want to let you know I'm onto you and I am sending the police over to break it up." Although I had a well-established reputation as a party girl at school I definitely didn't have the means to throw a party anywhere. I had heard of a few and was planning to attend at least one, but I had to rethink my plan. *Thank God I heard this message first*, I thought as I erased it before getting ready for the evening.

"You're not gonna believe this!" I said to Dana as I hopped into the backseat. "Sterling thinks I'm throwing a party. He left a voicemail saying he's going to bust me!"

"Shit, does that mean we shouldn't go tonight?" Dana was deflated as she was hardly ever let out of the house and I knew she and Dave wanted to get it on after prom. Her mom had snooped in her purse and found her birth control pills and then put her on lockdown.

"Let's see what happens tonight," I said, confident I could come up with a plan.

We went to the dorm to pick up the guys because they were both out-of-state students. They were called "dormies" at my school and Dana and I were "townies." Dave was from Boston and Roland was from Rhode Island. They were preppies and not my usual type to hang out with, let alone date, but I was doing this mainly for Dana, and to go to the prom. I also had a thing for the name Roland since Andy Gibb, my first crush, had been replaced with Roland Orzabal of Tears for Fears. I had fallen in love with him the summer before my thirteenth year when I heard him on the radio and he was my new future baby daddy, though I wanted nothing to do with having babies.

Dave had made a reservation at this really fancy restaurant, the kind where the waiter opens your napkin and puts it on your lap. I was immediately intimidated because I realized I didn't bring enough money. I was hoping to ask Mom for a few bucks but she still wasn't home when I left and the voicemail from Sterling threw me off my game so I forgot to grab the money I had stashed in my room. I was screwed. *Shit.* I wondered if my date was planning to pay, but a few minutes after sitting down Dana told me that Roland told Dave he didn't bring enough money either. "Okay, I'll just order a salad," I whispered back to Dana, not yet aware that even a salad was twenty-four dollars and I only had six bucks.

I was so worried about not having money to pay for my fancy salad (that tasted like potting soil) that I could hardly enjoy it. *Stupid, fucking rich kids,* I couldn't help thinking more than once. Dave was a nice guy but he came from money which is why he didn't bat an eye picking that restaurant in the first place. I certainly couldn't call myself poor anymore after Mom married Larry, but with my own money struggles I still always felt like I lacked. I found myself praying to Jesus over food once again, although this time it was a silent prayer in my head and the words were a little different:

Dear Jesus, please allow me to somehow pay for this wretched salad that I would not want my worst enemy to eat. This curly lettuce shit is awful and I'm not sure what these mushy yellow things are but they taste like they came out of an earthworm's asshole. You've always come through for me when I've prayed about food, Lord, so I know you will help me with this. Please God, please God, please God....

"Hey," Dana leaned over and whispered, interrupting my silent prayer. "Dave's going to pay for your salad. He says don't worry about it." The biggest wave of relief washed over me. Jesus came through for me once again. It wasn't Devil Dogs or Sno Balls but I was relieved that I didn't have to wash dishes or get arrested and go to juvie in my nice dress for stealing a disgusting salad. If I was going to be arrested it was going to be for something worth it, like that party.

Prom itself was fairly fun. The location had a great dance floor and I loved to dance so that was exciting. I decided to ignore Roland since he had disgraced me at dinner. How could a boy think he was taking me out when he was unable to buy me dinner? It wasn't long before I caught sight of Sterling on the dance floor with his poor wife. I had no idea how she lived with that guy. He was as nerdy as they come with his horn-rimmed glasses, middle-aged dad bod and total lack of a personality. Other than those things he wasn't so bad for the most part, just another adult figure who didn't care about me.

I wondered if he would come up to me and say something but he didn't. I wondered if he wondered if anyone got his voicemail. I pretended to know nothing about it, and he didn't ask, though I caught him staring at me more than once. I considered for a moment that he could be another pervy adult with naughty thoughts about me, but he was probably the most vanilla man I knew. Watching those two dance I was convinced that they had sex with the lights off.

When it was time to head to the party Dana panicked.

"I can't go. If I get busted I'll be grounded forever."

Dana was a true goody-goody. She wanted to have fun and be careless but she was always so afraid of her parents. She had a step-dad much like mine. His name was Arnold and he was always yelling about something, typically with a beer in his hand. Dana's mom was always squawking and scowling about something too.

Dana never would have dared to tell her parents off like I did and I could never figure out why. Perhaps it had something to do with the fact that she didn't have a door to her room. Their house was always under some kind of construction and she had cardboard walls and a tattered curtain where the door should be, so she couldn't scooch her dresser up against the door and hide like I did. I wished she would stand up for herself here and there but she didn't have it in her.

"We can just go home," I said, feeling deflated. It was prom and I was yet to have anything to drink or kiss any boys.

"Are you sure you don't mind? I can drop you off at the party and you can find a ride home." Home was more than an hour away from any of the parties so I chose to skip out, since I'd most likely have to offer an intense make-out session to get a ride that far.

"No, I'll go home too." We dropped the boys off at one of the parties and went home. I was rather glad in the end, though incensed when I found out the next day that Sterling was full of shit and never busted any party. He bluffed and we fell for it.

When school ended Mom didn't make me go to Dad's for the entire summer. He was living in Iowa in the tiniest of towns in the middle of nowhere. His house was nice and had a pool but I didn't have any friends out there so all I ended up doing was lying by the pool every day, smoking, reading books and making myself drinks from Dad's liquor cabinet. Samantha and I would go shopping on occasion but she was busy doing her thing and I felt isolated. I still didn't have a driver's license so I couldn't drive myself into town.

The whole license thing was a story in itself. Why was it so hard to get a driver's license in the state of Maine? First, you had to mail in an application to get a test date, which took eight or more weeks. Then, the test date was scheduled at least another eight weeks out.

I was nervous to take the test the first time and convinced Jess to let me use her Mom's car so I didn't have to parallel park the Rust Puppy or Mom's giant station wagon.

Who knew it would be snowing the first time I took the test? The roads were slick but it was Maine and the roads always sucked. I did fine at first even though my heart was racing the entire time. The driving instructor was a crotchety old man named Stan Crandall who had a perma-frown and smelled like charcoal. He made me over-the-top nervous but I tried not to let on.

"Pull in over here," he said as he pointed to a spot on a hill between two cars. *Oh no, I have to parallel park*, I thought as the sweat formed between my legs. I hated sweating there because it smelled like tomato soup and made me feel like a stinkbug that gives off a terrible odor to protect itself when it's scared.

"Ok," I mumbled. I forgot nearly everything Mom had taught me. Being from New York Mom was an excellent parallel parker and the only thing I remembered was how she taught me to line up my side mirror with the car I was parking behind. *Oh yeah, I have to crank the wheel.* I remembered that a little too late since I was already backing up. Mrs. O'Toole's Audi was large and the turning radius wasn't great; I'm not sure what else happened but long story short I tapped the car behind me.

"You just hit a parked car!" Stan yelled. I was hoping I had hit the curb but no such luck. "You fail!" His face turned purplish like Larry's. "Drive back to the station." I was in full-on panic mode by this point but I had to do what I was told so I drove back at a whole six miles per hour just to make sure I didn't hit any more cars, or pedestrians for that matter.

"Did you pass?" Jess asked as I got out of the car.

"Not this time." I just wanted to get the hell out of there. I filled her in on the details in the car. "I don't mind driving you around." She liked having a sidekick. "You'll pass next time," she said as we celebrated my failure with a few tokes from a joint she had in the ashtray.

* * *

Summer was winding down and school was just around the corner. One Sunday Jess and I drove around in her dad's pickup truck to see if we could find something to do. We made ourselves screwdrivers for the road in some thermoses we found in her kitchen. For a second I felt a twinge of guilt, remembering back to the days of going to church or watching Jim and Tammy Faye but the guilt turned to indignation when I remembered all the money Mom gave to those crooks. I made a silent toast in my head that went something like *Screw you crazy liars, God is right here in this stainless steel thermos.* I sure wished someone had told me sooner.

We had gone all the way to New Hampshire to get breakfast and on our way back we crossed over the Denmark Bridge. We had crossed this bridge countless times, but that day there were two guys standing on the edge, shirtless, getting ready to jump into the water. As we were passing I locked eyes with the taller guy. He motioned for us to turn the car around. Somehow, he commanded it.

"Hey, turn around. That guy just motioned for us to come back." Jess didn't waste a moment turning the truck around and parking right on the bridge. It so happened that the taller guy approached her window and the other guy came over to mine.

"What are you ladies up to today?" the taller, intense guy asked, staring right into my soul.

"Just driving around." My heart skipped a beat. "What about you boys?"

"We're here from Boston, camping for the weekend," Intense guy answered. I'm sure Jess and Other guy must have felt left out, but I couldn't help it. Intense guy was mesmerizing. And I could definitely tell he was from Boston with that accent. A Southie, most likely.

"Do you girls wanna come hang out with us and drink some beers?" Intense guy asked. Jess and I looked at each other.

"Sure thing. We'll meet you under the bridge," she replied. As we pulled away we both started giggling, happy that our uneventful Sunday had taken an interesting turn.

When I got out of the truck Intense guy came over to my door.

"My name's Ed," he said as he stuck his hand out.

"Hi, I'm Sparrow." I shyly shook his hand. His gaze was so intense that I averted my eyes so he couldn't see into me completely. I caught a glimpse of his perfect body, and it didn't help that he still had tiny drops of water running down his chest. His *very* toned chest and abs. The man definitely worked out. His hair was wet so I couldn't tell what color it was, but his eyes were the most perfect combination of Ceylon-blue sapphire and sea foam green. He reminded me of that store manager who let me off for stealing, however this was different. Ed wasn't looking at me the way Dreamboat looked at a wayward teenager. He was looking at me like I was a woman. A beautiful woman he wanted. I could tell he was older than me but I didn't get that pervy vibe I had experienced in the past. This was legit. My body shivered.

"I'm Miles," Other guy said. He handed me a beer and belched loudly in my general direction. I could tell Ed was the brains of the duo. Miles was darker-skinned and his belly hung over his swim trunks. He looked Italian, or maybe Armenian but I didn't bother to ask. He oozed a Neanderthal vibe. Perfect for Jess.

"Thanks," I said as I grabbed the beer and opened it. *Yes, I'm definitely going to need a few of these to hold my own with Intense guy*, I thought as I took a long sip.

"Let's go for a walk," Ed said grabbing my hand and leading me down the beach. I glanced back at Jess to make sure she was okay with me leaving and she seemed fine, already through her first beer and well into the second. If anyone had to look out it was Miles, since she would be climbing him in a matter of minutes.

"So, Sparrow, how old are you?" Ed and I were walking barefoot in the sand, drinking our Busch lights. "I'm eighteen." *Shit. I just lied.* "How about you?" I said before he could ask any more questions.

"I'm twenty-three."

"Oh." His age didn't bother me a bit. The summer before I had briefly dated a twenty-five-year-old history teacher I'd met at a music festival. I somehow rationalized that it was okay because he wasn't *my* teacher. He was working at a campground for the summer that happened to be less than a mile from my house. Mason was attractive, well-read, played the guitar and liked to get high. He had a three-foot bong named Charlotte that he'd made out of PVC pipe. He made me read *Still Life with Woodpecker* and taught me how to sing the words to "Creeque Alley" as he played the guitar. He also taught me to enjoy going to third base, although he never made me come. When Mom found out she shipped me off to Dad's the next day. There went my summer romance.

"So, what are you in to?" Ed asked as if he really wanted to know. I told him the truth, that I was getting ready to be a senior in high school. I told him I wanted to study psychology, that I played the piano and I loved French culture and language. He seemed intrigued. He told me about his life growing up in Boston, how his dad died when he was twelve, and how he quit school in the eighth grade to help his mom take care of the family. In a roundabout way he admitted to being a street rat, stealing cars and getting into lots of trouble. I asked about the scar over his left eye and he told me he it was from a beer bottle and how he had gotten it in a random bar fight. With every story he told me I was more and more attracted to him. Did I really just meet someone tougher than me? The more he told me the safer I felt with him. I could tell he was a real protector and looked out for others just like I did. Perhaps there was someone out there who would actually look out for me? I dismissed that thought as something only a weak person would consider. But I couldn't deny I felt calm in his presence and like I could let my guard down and be... well, a girl, on the inside too.

As the day went on we talked and talked some more. We both discovered we believed in aliens, and Ed explained how he thought someday we would all turn some shade of green to protect ourselves from the harsh rays of the sun once our atmosphere was burned off by pollution. I found his theories thought-provoking and insightful. We wound up in the front seat of his car, a fairly large Delta 88 with one long vinyl front seat, still drinking beer, though neither of us was drunk.

After a while Ed leaned in to kiss me, and I felt it everywhere. I knew I was supposed to be right where I was, kissing this man. Things got more heated when he pulled away and gazed at me.

"I want you." He was breathing heavily.

"Me too," I whispered. I was ready to go there. Ed leaned over me and opened his glove box to grab a condom. I had no idea that boys kept those things in there, but obviously real men did. And he was definitely a real man. His hair had dried by now and I could see he had a little bit of gray in the front mixed in with the soft red that was his natural color. He was pretty young to have gray but the truth was it was sexy. I had never been attracted to a redhead before but his wasn't a flaming red and he didn't have any freckles on his face, though he had them on his toned arms and back.

He began kissing me again and his stubble scratched my face. I had never kissed a guy with that much facial hair before and I liked it. I'm sure he hadn't shaved for a few days at least since he was camping but I didn't mind. It felt like he was leaving his mark on me.

His hands made their way up my shirt though he didn't remove it. He was an expert at unhooking my bra one-handed, especially since we were rather cramped with him lying on top of me in the front seat. He took his time unbuttoning and removing my shorts, wiggling them over my very round ass— my consolation prize from Jesus since the rosebuds he gave me never truly blossomed.

I helped him remove his swim trunks which had mostly dried. He took a break from kissing me to put the condom on. I put my hand on him to make sure the condom was on all the way and to guide him inside me. I was shocked at how large he was and wondered if I had drunk enough beers to dull the pain I was about to endure. It took a few tries for him to enter me and when he did it took my breath away. The pain was intense but only lasted for a minute or so and then it felt amazing. I realized I was completely wet from all of our kissing and being so attracted to him. I had enjoyed sex before, especially with Alex, but this was different. This was a physical sensation I had never experienced. *Maybe this is an orgasm*, I thought as my legs started shaking. Ed's eye contact was intense and I tried hard to keep his gaze. I had never looked someone in the eye like this while having sex, especially in broad daylight.

Even though it lasted a while, it was over way too soon. He was vocal when he came, which I liked until I realized the windows were open and Miles and Jess were probably nearby. I didn't come but I was closer than I ever had been. After lying there breathing together for more than a few minutes he slowly got up and pulled his shorts back on. I didn't see what he did with the condom but I had purposely turned my head as I sat up to avoid that awkward moment.

When I had gotten myself together we got out of the car for some air. Not far from us, we noticed Jess sitting naked on the hood of the truck and Miles with his pants down going at it. Ed and I giggled and started on another walk to let them have their privacy. As we were leaving, Miles came running, shorts falling to his ankles as he tried to hold them up with one hand.

"Eddie, wait," he cried as he approached us. He pulled Ed to the side and tried to talk quietly, but I heard every word. "Hey, Big Ed, I'm a little drunk and my dick's not working. Think you could go over there and finish her off?" Ed and I both turned to look at Jess, who was lying naked and spread-eagled on the truck. She was looking over at the boys, waiting to see who was coming back over to service her.

"Get the fuck outta here, are you outta your fucking mind?" Ed yelled.

"Oh, well, I just thought..."

"Go finish her off yourself." Ed grabbed my hand and led me away toward the beach.

"Was he serious?" I asked when we were out of earshot. I wasn't born yesterday and I realized Miles wouldn't have asked the question if he didn't think it was possible to get a yes.

"He's fucking crazy. I would never do that." I wasn't sure if I believed him but in that moment it didn't matter. I was on a post-Big Ed high with this beautiful specimen of a man and I wasn't going to let Jess ruin my experience.

"How did you meet Miles, anyway?" I asked, wondering how the two of them ever became friends.

"We're childhood friends," he replied. It made sense. What could keep these two friends other than a sense of childhood loyalty? "Why, you don't like him?" Ed asked.

"Well, I think Miles's dad should have pulled out," I said before I could think twice. After what had just happened I thought Miles was a steaming pile of dog shit. I hated him and his hairy back. I hated how he had no class. I imagined he would probably wipe his ass with his mother's wedding dress if he were out of Charmin. He was *that* guy.

Ed chuckled and I was glad my sharp tongue had not offended him. I didn't mean to talk trash about his friend but he was one of the most sub-human people I had the displeasure of hanging out with in a while, not including family of course.

When it was time to leave Ed asked for my number and I wrote it down for him. He gave me a giant bear hug and a sweet kiss and within a moment he was gone, headed back to Boston. It was getting dark so Jess and I got in her truck and she took me home. We both laughed and talked about the day. I tried hard not to judge her for her lack of class. To her credit she thought Miles was a steamy dump as well and she hoped to never hear from him. Although I didn't share her sentiment as far as Ed, I still left my lovely experience at the beach that day since I was certain I'd never hear from him and there was no sense pining for someone two states away. It was hard enough getting over Alex and I didn't need to go down that road again. Screw long distance.

To my great surprise Ed waited the customary three days and then called.

"Do you know who this is?"

"No, I sure don't," I lied.

"It's Ed, from the other day," he said.

I'm sure every girl remembered him.

"Oh, hi." My heart was racing and my face got hot. "How are you?" I asked, trying to sound casual.

I can't believe he called.

"Good, and yourself?" He asked as if he cared.

"I'm good, thanks." For a moment I worried that we wouldn't have much to talk about since we had already hit such a high note on our first encounter. I was wrong. We fell right back into intriguing conversations about science, politics, religion and books we had read. Talking with him was easy and refreshing. We had a lot of similar views on things and I loved the sound of his deep, gravelly voice. I also loved hearing his accent, though it was thick. He said "kwa-dah" instead of quarter and "peet-sir" instead of pizza but it just made him all the more endearing.

Ed told me all about his job as an over-the-road truck driver and how much he enjoyed it. He suggested that maybe some time I could go along on a ride with him and see the country. It did sound like fun. He said being cooped up together like that was a great way to get to know each other. It sounded adventurous and Lord knows I needed a real adventure.

I realized toward the end of the call that things were headed in a good direction and I needed to tell him the truth— that I was only sixteen and not eighteen like I had told him at the river.

"Ed, I have something to tell you. I'm not really eighteen," I said, worried.

"What? How old are you?"

"Ummm... well... I... I'm only twelve." I wanted to freak him out. Perhaps this way it wouldn't be that big of a deal when I told him the truth.

"Oh, fuck... oh no. You gotta be kidding me!"

"Ease up," I said, giggling. "I'm kidding! I'm sixteen, almost seventeen."

"Oh my God you scared the shit outta me! Are you still going to be a senior this year?"

"Yes, of course."

"Aren't you a little young for that?"

"Yes, it's a long story."

"Thanks for telling me the truth. Are your parents gonna kill you for talking to someone my age?"

"Probably. But I'm not worried about it if you aren't." What did I care what Mr. and Mrs. Moron thought? If Mom was that upset she could have Dr. Robertson up her medication and perhaps switch to a stronger cigarette. No big deal.

"Well...I guess not," he replied, though I could tell he was thinking about it. There was definitely an age difference we couldn't ignore, but I wasn't going to worry about it for now. Plus I loved that he was older and wasn't a silly high school boy looking to get laid.

The call from Ed was the first of many. We couldn't get enough of each other and talked on the phone every chance we got. Sometimes he would get in from work at two am and I would program my alarm to go off so I could call him. We talked for hours and it didn't matter if I was tired the next day because I was in love. I couldn't find one thing I didn't like about this man. It was barely a month and I was smitten. He felt the same.

Ed sent me postcards from the road, which I looked forward to receiving.

"Who's Ed?" Mom asked one day as she handed me a postcard.

"Oh, just a friend." I wasn't ready to tell her what was going on. She still thought I was dating a guy named Trent, which technically I was. But he was in Nicaragua with his mom building homes for the poor through his church. His mom didn't like that we were dating because she found condoms in his room and flipped out, which was why they were away for the summer. School was coming up, however, and I had to end it with him. I felt terrible breaking his heart since he was such a nice guy, but I was certain I wanted to be with Ed.

I devised a plan to tell Trent. I was going to wait until after the first week of school because I didn't want to ruin the first week of his senior year. I also didn't want him to think I had been cheating on him all summer, though I was unfaithful that day at the river. I wasn't afraid of being honest but I did want to protect him. He really loved me and he didn't deserve to start back to school with a broken heart. It was going to suck big time.

I shared my plan with Jess since she was the only one who knew about Ed and what happened that day. She agreed that it was a good plan and she understood I wanted to make it as drama free as possible. I should have known everything would backfire.

Chapter 19

The first day of senior year was exciting. It was fun to see the friends who had gone home over the summer and it was liberating to know that this was my last year at that hellhole. High school and I just did not agree and I couldn't wait to be out of there. One more year.

Trent and I met up in the morning and he was thrilled to see me.

"I have something for you," he said, as he hugged and kissed me. "I'll give it to you later." I was happy to see him too, but it made the whole thing worse and made me feel so low. How could I tell him the truth? That I had hooked up with a random guy and then fell for him? That I promised to remain faithful and broke that promise? I pushed it out of my mind as I listened to tales of Nicaragua, how hot it was there, how hard he worked and so on. He did have a beautiful tan now on top of his gymnast's body. *Oh dear, did I make a mistake?* I liked this boy. I thought I'd take the week to decide. I was still obsessed with Ed but he was far away and even though we talked on the phone a lot he wasn't making any plans to visit me. It was a conundrum.

I told Jess about my dilemma and she understood.

"Yeah, just take the week and decide," she agreed. By this point I had also told Dana about my situation and I trusted her more than I trusted Jess.

"You're nuts," she said, shaking her head as I told her that Ed was twenty-three and divorced with two kids. "Larry and Joan are gonna flip their shit!" I couldn't make her understand that they were the least of my worries. I was almost seventeen and they couldn't lock me away. I didn't care about disappointing them at all. Larry had already told me on more than one occasion that I'd never amount to anything, so I didn't need his blessing regarding my choice of boyfriend. I wouldn't have gotten it anyhow.

That day after school Trent gave me my gift from Nicaragua, a bottle of authentic Nicaraguan spiced rum. I was expecting earrings or a bracelet, but I could understand why he bought me booze— because I really liked it and he was trying to please me.

"Oh, thanks," I said as I slipped the bottle into my backpack. I gave him a quick kiss and was off, riding home with Jess.

"I feel so bad, Jess. Trent brought me back a bottle of rum."

"Really? Let's crack it."

"No, I should hold onto it. In case he wants it back."

"What are you gonna do?"

"I have to tell him. I just have to." I was going to tell him over that upcoming weekend so he could process it before going back to school. I couldn't drag it on any longer.

The next day at school was uneventful. I had decided to buckle down and study hard, seeing as it was my final year there and I wanted it to be a success. I had signed up for an advanced placement anatomy class I was excited about, though less so when they brought us cats to dissect. The smell alone was one thing, but having to skin a very stiff dead cat with its mouth gaping open and its eyes crossed was a whole other crisis. I looked around the room and realized all the cats looked the same, like they were sent to a gas chamber and had died a horrible, horrible death.

"I can't do this," I told my partner Emily as we were putting our gloves on and getting ready to literally skin a cat.

"I know, it's gross, but we'll get through it," she said.

And with that she started skinning as if she were cutting the fat off a chicken preparing it for dinner. I blinked back the tears welling up in my eyes and followed suit. Even though I had grown to loathe cats when one pissed in my closet and ruined all the clothes that were on the floor I still felt bad for this unfortunate kitty, which turned out to have a half-digested mouse in his belly. *Well, at least he didn't die hungry* was all I could think as I skinned away, peeling back his formaldehyde-soaked black-and-white fur. Some of the guys in class were standing their kitties up and making them dance, like it was some big joke. It irritated me and just confirmed I was done with high school boys. It was time to date a real man.

At the end of the day I waited outside for Trent. He looked really angry and when I tried to say hi he cut me off.

"Is it true?"

"Is what true?" I asked, a lump in my throat.

"Did you cheat on me this summer? Is there someone else?" I had never seen Trent so angry and hurt at the same time. His eyes were glassy and his face was red. His brow was creased and he was shaking.

"Who told you that?" I asked, horrified because I already knew the answer.

"Who do you *think?*" he yelled. "Is it true?"

"I did meet someone this summer and I was going to tell you but I wanted to wait a bit. I didn't want to ruin your first week of school." Tears started falling.

"Did you fuck him? *Did* you?" He grabbed my arm a little too hard.

"Yes."

"I can't believe you! You bitch!" he screamed as he let go of my arm.

"I'm so sorry..." I grabbed his arm to get him to look at me. "Can we talk about this?"

"No! And don't ever talk to me again!" He yelled as he walked away.

By this time a small crowd had gathered to see what we were fighting about. I was sure this would get around the school in a day or so and then everyone would know. I knew Jess had told him. Why was she such a horrible friend?

I tried to find her to cuss her out this time but she was nowhere to be found. I knew I'd see her eventually and would give it to her. I was so sick of her shit, sick of someone pretending to be my friend. Screw her. I meant it this time.

The next day I found Jess over by the lockers. I had heard through friends that she and Trent were hanging out now and I wondered if she thought they would date. I found solace in the fact that I knew he wouldn't date her due to her horrible reputation but I was sure she was cozying up to him, hopeful.

"What the hell is your problem?" I yelled as I banged my hand on the locker by her head. "Why would you do this to me?"

"What are you talking about?" she asked, averting her gaze.

"I know you told Trent about Ed."

"No I didn't!"

"Jess, I know it was you. He told me."

"You're crazy," she said, turning to walk away. She couldn't even face me. I finally decided then and there that I was done with Jessica O'Toole, once and for all.

School was a disaster for the next few weeks as Trent would yell things at me when he saw me in the hall. Surprisingly, it didn't wreck me. I was a senior now, making changes. Dating an older man was helping me evolve. Ed didn't like cigarettes so I cut down to almost none. I also stopped drinking and smoking weed for the most part. I started doing my homework. Ed would call and sometimes stay on the phone with me until it was done. I would read him the assignments and he'd give me ideas on how to answer, though he never did it for me. Ed didn't go to high school so I think he was living through me a little. It was fun. I had never had so much support and I didn't want to disappoint him. He was bringing out the best in me.

Being away from Jess was a huge step in the right direction. I wasn't skipping school anymore, or living to party and get drunk on weekends. I was beginning to think about my future. I decided I wanted to go to college in Florida, so I could be by the water. Then maybe after I graduated I could spend some time in France. Ed loved that idea and said he would support me any way he knew how. It felt like we were becoming a thing and I was over the moon.

"Who the hell is calling Boston at all hours of the night?" Larry yelled as he tore through the house, phone bill in hand. *Shit.* I had forgotten about the phone bill. I had no idea how much it cost to call long distance so many times but evidently it was a lot. "Who are you calling?" he asked again, this time after he burst into my room. I was lying on my bed doing homework and I looked up at him with a blank stare.

"Is it bad?" I asked. "I thought I only called a few times."

"It's three hundred dollars! And why are you calling anyone at two am?"

At that point I realized I was going to have to tell the truth. I hated lying anyway, not to mention I felt like things with Ed and me were getting pretty serious and I wanted the world to know, even if my world contained a few trolls.

"The truth is I have a new boyfriend and he lives in Boston. I'm sorry about the phone bill. I'll be more careful in the future." I tried to sound respectful and business-like because I was so sick of the drama. Perhaps if I apologized he would calm down and discuss it rationally. No such luck.

"You are forbidden from using the phone! You're grounded!" Larry screamed, slamming the door on his way out. Too bad he was back from his crop dusting season because Mom would have paid the bill without even looking at it. This time of year was always the pits since Larry felt the need to assert himself as the authority in the house because he was gone for most of the spring and summer, kind of like a dog that lifts his leg on the same chair or attacks other dogs to assert dominance. Larry needed to be the wolf in charge.

"What's this I hear about a new guy?" Mom asked when she heard about the phone bill.

"Yeah, I met him over the summer. He's great," Mom wasn't involved in my life but she was still nosy.

"What happened to Trent?"

"We broke up, Mom. It happens."

"Oh. I thought you really liked him," Mom said, disappointed. The truth was Mom liked Trent because he had an Italian last name. As a matter of fact when Larry was gone she sometimes let him spend the night on weekends. More than once he slept in my room and Mom either didn't notice or didn't care. She knew we were doing it because she asked.

"Does he have an Italian schlong?"

That was Mom after a few drinks mixed with her pills.

"Mom! How would I know? He's my first Italian boy." I was horrified that we were talking about the size of my boyfriend's dick.

"Well, typically Italian boys are well-endowed, and they usually aren't circumcised."

"Mom, stop!" Trent was circumcised but Mom didn't need to know. I had seen an uncircumcised penis once on this guy named Trey. I was in Alabama at chubby cousin Darla's wedding. Some guys at the rehearsal dinner asked if I wanted to go to a party and I said yes. So off I went with six boys, several of them groomsmen. After the party a few of them wanted to go cow tipping. Being an East Coast girl that was new to me but I was tipsy and game, though I never actually tipped a cow because that's just too goddamned mean. Instead Trey and I went off to make out and next thing I knew he's whipping his pants off and there it was, basking in the moonlight— a shiny pink miniature elephant trunk that shimmered under a bright moonbeam.

"Would you like to touch it?" Trey asked, as if his dick were a real treasure, like a newborn panda or a congressional medal of honor.

"Oh, no thanks," I replied, trying to sound gracious as if someone were offering me pickled herring and I didn't want to offend that person by saying I loathed pickled herring. I may have been a bit more curious if I had felt better, but things started spinning and I felt a pain in my stomach. *Oh no, here it comes.* I heaved a few times and then it all came up— every French fry and tequila shot I had ingested that evening. I mostly puked on the ground between us but I definitely sprayed Trey and me, including my legs and his crotch. Orange, chunky, smelly puke. *Why is it orange for fuck's sake? Oh yeah, ketchup.*

"God, I'm so sorry," I said as I wiped my face with the back of my hand.

"It's okay." Trey jumped up and put his Jackson Pollocked trunk away in record time. "Maybe some other time. Let's get you home." He walked me to the car and helped me in. *Those poor, sweet cows,* was all I could think before I closed my eyes and passed out.

"Mom, I did like Trent. It's just that I met someone I like more." Mom sat on my bed to hear more which was something she never did. Mom never came in my room, at least not when I was in it. She wasn't angry about the phone bill and she appeared genuinely interested in what was going on in my love life. She had probably just popped a pill or three, but I decided to spill it anyway.

"Mom, Ed's a little bit older than me but we've talked about it and we are both okay with it. He's responsible, mature and he really likes me."

"How old is he, Sparrow?"

Here goes.

"He's twenty-three, Mom."

"What? No, Sparrow, that's too old." Mom got up from my bed and went right back into control freak mode.

So much for a mother-daughter moment.

"You need to end it with him immediately," she added as she wagged her finger in my face.

"Mom, I'm not doing that," I replied, calmly. I was enjoying my new found self-control. I was going to stand my ground without yelling, screaming or insulting anyone. At least I was going to try.

"I'm not having this discussion with you," Mom said. "You're giving me chest pains!"

And with that she turned and left, no doubt to pop yet another Xanax or light a cigarette. Probably both. Leave it to Mom to melt over something so minor. I wasn't pregnant or on heroin. I wondered what Dr. Robertson would have prescribed if I had been.

Mom couldn't deal with the reality of my new love interest so she sent Larry into my room to do her dirty work. Twice in one day! Larry typically never entered my room because he wasn't allowed. Once he had come upstairs to use the bathroom in the middle of the night and had opened the door to my room to discover I had sneaked out. This was something I did on occasion until junior year My room was on the second floor and I would carefully climb through my window, hang by my hands and jump to the ground. These were evenings I couldn't barricade my door because I wouldn't be able to get back in. I was in massive trouble when I came home but the critical part was the fact that Larry was peeking into my room in the first place. My mind went to dark places based on past experiences.

"What's this I hear about you dating an older man?" Larry asked.

"What about it?" I replied, not looking up from my book.

"An older guy like that only wants to get in your pants, Sparrow! He doesn't care about you."

"He's not like that. He really does care."

"Bullshit! Wake up, he's using you. You're not allowed to date him, do you hear me?" Larry slammed the door as he left.

Normally I would have gotten up off my bed and fought back, saying shocking and hurtful things like, "Well, he already got in my pants and he's still calling so I guess I'm good at something!" or, "Did you ever consider that maybe I wanna get in *his* pants?" But I refrained. I wanted to take this seriously and knew that I would have to be the mature one. I couldn't let my temper get in the way because I wanted Ed to be able to pick me up and actually date me. I wouldn't have even told Larry and Mom how old he was except for the fact that he actually looked thirty-three not twenty-three and if I didn't mention it they would have freaked out on a whole different level, probably calling the police and finally hauling my ass off to juvie.

"So, my parents freaked out when I told them how old you are," I told Ed one night on the phone. "They think you just want to get in my pants."

"Oh no, really? That sucks. Why don't I spend some time with your parents when I see you and explain my intentions."

I was shocked he would even put himself in that position. *Maybe this guy really does care for me*, I thought. He sure was acting like it. I was working on Mom, telling her nice things Ed said to me here and there, but she wasn't buying it. I couldn't believe that with all the freak show moments my family had they would overreact to the age difference. Mom went on about how Dr. Robertson and Donald both thought it was a horrible idea for me to date someone so much older. I wondered what they would think if they knew he was divorced with two kids, but I would have slit my wrists before telling her that. They probably would have chained me up in the basement or God knows what. I wasn't about to find out.

Not long after that conversation I sat Mom and Larry down and told them I had something to discuss with them. I'm sure at least one of them thought I was pregnant, especially since Mom refused to let me take birth control pills, even though my periods were horrid and she knew I was doing it on occasion.

"Use a condom like we do," Mom said once when I was nagging her about it. She and Larry used Trojan Lambskin condoms and I knew this because for one thing I snooped and found them and for another thing she used to get them at the local Shop and Save along with our weekly groceries. She threw them in the cart right alongside the milk and Devil Dogs. I guess Larry was too afraid to get his balls cut.

"Ed would like us to invite him over so he can meet you both and explain that he is not just looking to get in my pants." I could tell they were both surprised by this request. "If you don't like him after meeting him then we can talk, but I think you owe it to me to give him a chance."

"I don't know..." Larry shook his head. I think Mom's curiosity got the better of her.

"I think it would be okay if we had him over for dinner, don't you, Larry?"

Larry thought for a moment.

"Fine, but he's not taking you anywhere. You two are staying here."

"Sure, no problem," I said as I darted off to my room to call Ed and tell him. I had a secret phone I had found in Punky's closet that I was able to plug into the phone jack in my room. I knew I'd be found out at some point, but at the time I was in the clear.

I was nervous the day Ed was coming to meet my parents. I spent the majority of the day doing dishes, vacuuming and picking up toys. I scrubbed the bathroom. I was thankful I had just painted the bathroom ceiling since it had turned completely green from mold since the fan in the bathroom broke and Larry never bothered to fix it. I had watched as the mold started as a small patch in one corner of the ceiling, and then spread until it covered the whole damned thing. I asked Mom if we were going to get sick and die because I'd heard of molds killing people, plus I was allergic to penicillin which is a type of mold. Mom insisted people only got sick from black mold and this was green so it wouldn't bother us. When I took a shower with the door closed it felt like I was trapped inside a moldy loaf of Wonder bread and I imagined the mold getting into my lungs and leaving spores that would spread and take over until one day I collapsed. The alternative, showering with the door open, was totally unacceptable. I preferred to take my chances with the mold.

Ed came in through the back door and shook Mom's hand. Mom had put on a fancy sweater and a full face of makeup and was talking in a syrupy voice that I hadn't heard in eons.

"Hi Ed, nice to meet you. Would you like a beer?" she asked.

"Uh, no thank you," he replied, shooting me a puzzled look.

What was Mom up to, I wondered. She caught us looking at one another and said, "Well, he *is* old enough, Sparrow." I ignored her and offered Ed a seat at the breakfast bar, which was our only table. It was a double-sided bar with three stools on each side and it separated the kitchen from the living room. Larry had made the bar himself by cutting a section out of the wall and putting a giant slab of wood in that he had stained and lacquered. The table was shiny but the wood was easily dented being pine, so every time someone wrote on a piece of paper while sitting at the breakfast bar it was forever etched into the table. I was the first to recognize this and several years earlier had spent hours writing profanities on pieces of paper pressing real hard, knowing they would be carved into the table forevermore. Larry soon noticed and was upset but it was entirely his fault. He should have sprung for a harder wood. Thank goodness for placemats.

Mom made a pasta dish for dinner which reminded me of my birthday with Morris and how he was my first real date. Edward was my second older man. He hadn't brought me flowers like dear Morris but he did do a great job of fielding questions from Mom and Larry. He told them about his job as a truck driver, all about living in Boston and most important, what his intentions were.

"I really like your daughter and I'd like to date her," he told both of them. His candor caught them off guard and neither knew how to respond. "I know we have a slight age difference but I think we can all be mature and get past it," he added.

"You seem like a nice guy, Ed, but we'll have to think it over," Larry said, as if his opinion mattered one iota.

"I understand," Edward replied, unfazed.

I chose to ignore their back and forth because Ed was handling himself like a champ. It made me like him even more, especially since I could just sit back and let him handle stuff like that. I didn't have to be on the alert or defend myself in any way. I could relax and just be. This was a brand new experience.

As the night wore on Edward won my family members over one by one. He helped clear dishes. He played with Doodie. He chatted with Punky. He even engaged Larry in conversation about flying since his dream was to someday become a pilot.

"I like your family," Ed said when I walked him to his car later on.

"Are you joking? You don't have to say that." I was embarrassed that he had witnessed the freak show.

"No, they're pretty nice. I can tell your step dad is leery of me, though. He kept looking at me sideways."

"I'm sorry." I thought of ways to torture the troll later. I had been meaning to get my hands on some Nair for his shampoo, since he was always concerned about his ever-growing bald spot. The thought of hearing screams from the shower and envisioning clumps of hair rushing down the drain eased my anxiety.

"Trust me; I can handle a guy like that. Don't you worry," he said as he kissed my head and gave me a giant bear hug, lifting me off the ground. "I'll call soon." Ed hopped in his car and took off, leaving me standing in an ethereal mix of oxytocin and exhaust fumes.

I never knew what soon meant but I stayed on that head-kiss high for days afterward. I couldn't believe I had finally met my soul mate only to suffer the fate of him living hours away. Why was the universe so cruel?

After that pivotal day was when the longing started. I thought about Edward Joseph McCue twenty-four hours a day. I floated through my days in a state of bliss that would have made Eros himself throw up in his mouth a little. Instead of writing murder plots or I-hate-you letters in my dear diary I started writing love poems. Me, the girl who insisted that anyone who wrote poetry was either bipolar or schizophrenic. My poems were beyond sappy. They all rhymed perfectly which was a dead giveaway that I wasn't meant to be a poet, much like how Dad was never meant to be a surgeon.

Ed started calling more. And coming to visit.

"Hey, I'm gonna come see you this weekend," he said one Sunday night on the phone. I was up late coloring various drawings of a cell for anatomy and Ed was staying on the phone with me until I got it done.

"That seems like so far away!" I couldn't wait to see his face and smell him again and run my fingers through his baby fine hair and stare into his blue lagoons and count the endless freckles on his forearms. But I had to wait an entire week; how would I deal?

"It'll go by before you know it. Just make sure your parents let you out of your cage, okay?"

"I'll take care of it," I promised before hanging up, which was always an ordeal. It usually took us at least ten minutes to end a call and it was both our faults. We hated hanging up and Ed always tried to make me hang up first but I never could, at least not before six or seven times which probably made it all the more painful.

I have read that it takes seven times to quit an addiction and I completely believe it, because I was already addicted to Ed, but that was an addiction I was perfectly happy keeping. The Marlborough Lights could take a hike.

Chapter 20

I breezed through the week, ecstatic that I was going to see Ed on Friday. The truth is I labored through painfully picking off the days, hours, and sometimes minutes. Mom gave in and said he could pick me up and take me on a real date. I'm not sure how she convinced Larry but I didn't dare ask because I was too smart to rock the boat.

I planned my outfit days in advance and made sure my eyebrows were perfect. After an intense round of plucking to turn thick, Italian caterpillars into thin, Asian butterfly antennae, I sprayed my brow brush with Mink, the best hair spray ever in those days, and expertly brushed them into place. Those things weren't going to move all night, no matter what kind of shenanigans I got up to.

I was excitedly nervous when Ed came to the door. I was glad I had slathered on extra deodorant because I instantly broke into a sweat. This was dinner, not the prom, but my nervous system said otherwise.

"Hi dahlin', look at you," Ed said as he scooped me up for one of his bear hugs. I melted into him and held on like my life depended on it. When I finally broke away Ed went over and hugged Mom.

"Have fun," she said cheerfully as we left. Luckily for us she was smitten with Ed herself. He was the kind of person that everyone wanted to be around, like some kind of human magnet.

"Where are we going tonight?" I asked as we were driving down the road, holding hands and talking about our week.

"I thought we would do dinner first and then see," Ed replied, smiling. He seemed just as excited to see me which warmed my insides. I wondered what we would do after dinner, feeling guilty that I wasn't old enough to go to a bar or go dancing like women his age. In an instant I went from feeling elated to feeling small. *What does he see in me?* I wondered, feeling like a little girl playing dress up. I looked down at my cream-colored floral shirt and jeans. Even though I was a smart dresser for the sticks I was convinced that Boston girls way out-classed me and let's face it— their rosebuds were probably in full bloom.

I was still feeling self-conscious as we entered the steak house, but my insecurity faded as I sat across from Ed and held his hand at the table. I ordered a Sprite and he got a beer, and we sat and talked about everything under the sun. Government, politics, religion, all the things we talked about during those late night phone conversations. We were still on the same page about everything, which was enchanting. Then it took an interesting turn.

"So, whose car are you driving?" I asked when he grabbed his keys and started playing with them at the table. He had picked me up in a sporty red two-door which was a far cry from the Delta 88 but I was so excited to see him I had forgotten to ask.

"Oh, uh, it belongs to a friend." Ed looked uncomfortable. Just then I happened to notice the key chain and it was distinctly feminine.

"Is this friend a girl?" My stomach hit the floor.

"Uh...yeah." Edward shifted in his seat, well, squirmed was more like it.

I got the big picture. *Shit. Shit Fuck. Dammit!*

"You're seeing her, aren't you?" I was pinching my hand under the table so I wouldn't cry. A useful trick I had learned years ago in grade school when Mrs. Hatch yelled at me.

"Well, yes, I have been. I guess we haven't talked about being exclusive," he added, as if that made driving hours to see me in another woman's car less egregious.

"No, I guess we haven't." I pushed down the anger and sadness attempting to engulf me with one giant gulp of air. Instead of crying, or yelling or storming out like I wanted to I looked away and played with my soda straw, pushing it in and pulling it out of the glass as if it were less boring than our conversation.

"Hey, look at me." Ed grabbed my face and brought it up to eye level. "I'm breaking it off with her when I get back. I would have done it sooner but I wanted to borrow the car," he said in his best Boston accent, which didn't get to me at all until he said "caaaaah."

"Oh really?" I turned my head, nose in the air. "And what's this girl's name?" I just had to know.

"Her name's Trish."

Trish. Trish? It pissed me off that he didn't say her full name. Like her parents really named her Trish. Her name was probably Tricia, or Patricia, but he called her Trish. Why? Because he was banging her? Because they were homies? He sure did seem comfortable playing with those keys, just like they were his.

"Well, she's awfully nice to let you borrow her car. Are you sure you want to just drop her like that?" He deserved the sarcasm.

"Aww, come on, don't be like that. Trish is a very nice girl but I'm breaking up with her for one reason." Ed grabbed my hand.

Ugh. There's that tingly feeling again.

"What's this big reason?" I asked, still unable to look him in the eye.

"I'm ending it with her because I want to be with you." Ed grabbed my other hand firmly and clasped them both together. "I want you to be my girl, Sparrow. Please say yes." His gaze was intense and I was no match for it. He had superpower heat ray vision and was boring into me, melting the years and years of ice that had formed in parts of my heart I didn't know existed. Now I knew what people meant when they said they turned into a puddle. Was I going to let him have this much control over me?

"Of course I'll be your girl." Trish who? At that moment I was the only girl alive, certainly the only girl Ed had ever laid eyes on.

"Come on, let's get outta here." Ed paid the check and ushered me out before I could blink twice.

"Where are we going?" I asked once we had made it to the car.

"You'll see,"

He was so cool and in control. I looked over and wanted to run my fingers through his hair while he was driving but I decided against it. Where was he taking me? I was clueless, until we pulled in.

"I got us a room, babe, so we can have some time alone." Ed jumped out to come around and open my car door. I half-smiled as he grabbed my hand and pulled me out of the car. The Motor Inn. I had passed this place dozens of times over the years and had never considered that one day I would venture inside.

"I've already checked in, our room is this way." Ed grinned as he guided me to room 102.

The room was small but decent. The decor was eighties but so were the times. Ed had gone to the liquor store earlier and picked up some beers.

"You want one?" he asked as he popped a top.

"Yeah, sure." I took one from him, thankful that he had gotten bottles instead of cans.

"Come talk to me." Ed plopped onto the bed and his hand patted where he wanted me to sit.

"What do you want to talk about?" I asked, smiling, already feeling the Bud Light kicking in. I climbed on the bed and laid my head on his shoulder. How could I have thought about being angry at this man for even a moment? It was obvious he went to so much trouble to come see me and now I was his girl. What's her face will be gone as soon as he returns that car. *Wait, why did he have to borrow her car in the first place?* I decided I didn't need to know. I wasn't going to wreck this magic moment.

Ed didn't want to talk at all. He grabbed my face and leaned in to kiss me. I felt it everywhere and knew where this was going. I was thankful I was fully groomed and shaved in all the right places. I had hoped this moment would happen and was relieved it wasn't in a car again, especially since the car belonged to that girl, not to mention it had bucket seats, which I couldn't imagine would be any kind of comfortable.

Ed unbuttoned my shirt, taking his time with each button. He was almost too gentle, as if I were a doll and he didn't want to break me. Part of me relished his soft touch and the other part of me wanted him to be more forceful. He brought out something primal in me and I didn't want to hold it back. I had been trying hard for months to hold back the intensity of my anger and disappointment at home and I wanted to be able to let myself go with Ed. Why did he make my heart beat so fast? Why did he make me more than a little dizzy when he smiled at me? When he kissed me I knew he would be the last man I shared DNA with.

I was convinced this was what love was. It had to be. I thought I had been in love with Alex but realized I *felt* loved, which was amazing, but there was no way I could have been in love with him when I didn't have these physical sensations. Or maybe it was a peaceful kind of love, which was something I knew nothing about. This thing with Ed was anything but peaceful. In fact it was the opposite of peaceful; it was frenetic. Every single one of my cells did a dance when he touched me. I thought I was a terrible kisser because when he kissed me I almost stopped breathing. I was afraid I'd hyperventilate so I pulled away before I wanted to for fear of having a full on panic attack on his face. But tonight was different. I was ready to go there, and the Bud Light was helping.

I shagged Edward like it was the last time I would ever see him. *I'll bet even Trish doesn't do it like this,* I thought more than once. I grabbed his face, licked his ears, bit his neck and even clawed his back a little. I didn't make it on top of him but it didn't matter. I definitely proved my skills worthy in the bedroom, well, one-room motel, but *still*. I wore his ass out.

"Wow, Sparrow." He had just rolled off me and was lying on his back breathing hard. I enjoyed watching his chest go up and down with each breath and was proud that I had turned him into a mouth breather. I didn't come but I was close and that was good enough for me. I guess I wasn't ready to fully let myself go, but I knew I would be one day.

Ed got up to dispose of the condom and clean himself off. When he came back I snuggled into his chest and ran my fingers through his chest hairs. He didn't have many but most of them were already gray. I chalked it up to his tough childhood and briefly wondered if I was going to go gray myself soon.

"I need to get you home," Ed said.

"I know," I whispered, not wanting the night to end. I wanted to enjoy every moment with this man. This was just like talking on the phone and not being able to hang up only worse because our naked bodies were stuck together and I had no idea how to unstick them.

"What's that smell?" Edward asked, suddenly, as he lifted his head and stuck his nose in the air, sniffing like a dog that smells a steak cooking. "Did you fart?" he asked, laughing. Only he said "faht" in that thick Boston accent that somehow made the word even more offending.

"No, of course not!" I was aghast. I definitely didn't fart, but if I had I would have still denied it. But now I was mortified that he actually thought I did. "Smell my ass," I offered as I turned and shoved it in his face. "See? Roses," I added, before realizing that it was just his clever way of unsticking us. Sometimes even real men revert to boyish tactics, I suppose.

It worked. My chemical romance high was dulled instantly and I got up to get dressed.

"Yeah, I had better get home," I said, though I would have given anything to stay and fall asleep on Ed's chest, at the Motor Inn on the hardest, creakiest bed I had ever shagged on.

The car ride home was mostly silent. We held hands and I dozed off a few times, doing that bobble-head thing you do when you are trying to stay awake so the other person doesn't fall asleep while driving.

"Hey, Miss Sparrow, we're here," Edward said, gently touching my shoulder.

Damn, I fell asleep after all.

"I had a great time tonight." He leaned in and kissed my forehead before getting out to walk around and open my door. We held hands as he walked me to the back door and gave me one of his famous lift-me-off-the-ground bear hugs. "I'll call ya soon, babe," he whispered in my ear as he put me back down.

"Okay," I mouthed, smiling yet choking back some tears. I hated watching Ed drive away. It literally created a pain in my heart and made it hard to breathe. *This love thing is intense,* I thought as I let myself in and bee-lined to the bookcase in the living room. Mom had some books about love and relationships and I needed to learn more about what was happening to me.

Chapter 21

It didn't take long to confirm I was definitely in love with Ed. Hopelessly, madly in love with the man. It was unsettling because I didn't know exactly how he felt about me. I knew he liked me, but clearly he was seeing another girl. Would he really stop dating her? I wasn't adept at trusting anyone, let alone boys, let alone adults, let alone *men*. I didn't like how this love thing was taking control of me. Sure I had been boy crazy before, but this was different. This was unraveling me.

I did what any level-headed girl who wanted to keep herself intact would do; I dated other guys. I was still getting attention from boys at school and until Edward professed his undying love for me, it was still open season. Sure I had agreed to be his "girl" but he hadn't used the "L" word so technically I was still single. Kind of. In any event I was still going to date boys and maybe kiss them but I definitely wouldn't shag them or even come close. But I would keep myself distracted enough so that if Ed broke my heart it wouldn't completely wreck me. It sounds crazy now but it made sense at the time.

The first guy I set my sights on was a Sicilian boy named Lance. I'm not sure who named him Lance and why he wasn't a Luigi or an Angelo because he sure looked the part. He was dark-skinned with jet black hair and was the hairiest boy at school. I didn't get any kind of butterflies around him, which was perfect since my heart was already taken. Lance dumped me pretty quickly, however, after being at a party one night where he tried to shag and I said no, grazi. I was sticking to the deal in my head that I would "date" boys but not sleep with them. Besides, Lance smelled just like my grandpa, which was a major turnoff. They were the same ethnicity and I had read somewhere once that if someone's smell turns you off it means that your genes are too much alike and you shouldn't procreate because you could end up with a three-headed baby. Even if I hadn't been in love with Ed I couldn't possibly have done it with Lance because what if the condom broke and I ended up with a three-headed Monchhichi?

The next guy who grabbed my attention was James Davidson. James had blond, curly hair, pale skin and was on the wrestling team—the exact opposite of my type, which also made him perfect. We had some of the same friends and found ourselves hanging out together on occasion. One night I was with my new friend Amy and we were picking up some kids to go to a party. We picked up James first and he asked Amy to pick up everyone else while he and I would walk over to the gym and meet up with everyone there.

James suggested we walk through the cemetery on the way to the gym and I agreed. It was an old cemetery dating back to the 1700s and I was never sure why it was on school grounds. There weren't any street lights so it was dark but my eyes soon adjusted and I could at least see a little in front of me. We found a bench and sat so we could drink the beers I had stuffed in the pockets of some very baggy pants I was wearing. We talked about it being our senior year and what our plans were after graduation. After a few minutes he leaned over to kiss me and I let him. I was enjoying making out with someone who didn't agitate my cells. I almost preferred not feeling anything to the intensity I had with Ed.

Before long James tried to put his hand up my shirt and I stopped him. "Hey, let's take this slow," I said, grabbing his hand and putting it back on his lap. Before I knew what was happening he threw me down on the ground and in a millisecond had his penis out and in my face, trying to force it in my mouth. I was on my back, lying on someone's headstone, which I had hit my head on, but not hard enough to make me stop thinking. *Shit, how am I gonna get out of this?* I fought James off with all my might.

I kept turning my head to avoid his dick, still in shock that this was happening with someone I considered a friend. When he realized I wasn't going to eat it he quickly changed to plan B and ripped my zipper open to go for the gold. As soon as he took his hands off my arms I reached around on the ground to see what I could find to throw at him. I grabbed a handful of dirt and threw it in his face, which meant it went in my face too but I closed my eyes and turned my head, so he got most of it. He sat up to rub his eyes, giving me time to feel around and find a good-sized rock that I used to bash his right temple. I bashed hard.

At this point he was dazed enough for me to roll out from underneath him and claw my way to freedom. I was agile and on my feet before he knew what was happening. I ran just as fast as that day in the swamp when I thought Dad was going to blow me to bits and I felt like a superhero jumping over some headstones and running around others. I briefly wondered if there were any ghosts hanging around watching this horror show. I never looked back and didn't stop running until I came to the entrance of the gym, where everyone was waiting.

"What happened to you?" Amy asked, picking leaves and twigs out of my hair. I was breathing hard and couldn't catch my breath enough to answer, so I stood there panting like a dog.

"Whoa, that was a close one, wasn't it, Sparrow?" James said, also panting.

Oh my fucking stars he followed me.

"The cops pulled in and we decided to run from them, right Sparrow?" I looked around at my six friends, all staring at me, one of them being Trent, my ex. There was no way I was going to tell all these people what really happened.

"Yeah, that was a close one," I said, not lying.

"Really, Sparrow?" Trent pointed to my wide-open broken zipper. "Nice," he added, as he walked away, shaking his head. Trent thought I was in the cemetery shagging James. Could this be any worse?

I tried to cover it up with some ridiculous story about how I was trying to pee and my zipper broke but it was clear everyone thought James and I did it. *Fucking great.* On top of that I had to spend the evening with a would-be rapist, pretending everything was just peachy.

"Who wants to smoke a bowl?" I asked, changing the subject. I happened to have some weed in my purse, and we all piled into Amy's car and got high. The worst part was that wanker smoked my bud.

I realized that my brilliant plan of dating other boys was just a waste of time and could possibly get me knocked up or worse, so I gave in to love and focused exclusively on Ed. He never would have treated me like a piece of meat or tried to hurt me in any way. I never reported James to school or to the authorities, which was a total mistake. I only told one friend who thought I had better keep my mouth shut or else I would ruin my reputation. I decided he was probably right. I didn't tell Ed because I think he would have murdered the kid, who I later found out was totally tripping on acid that night. Or at least that was the story.

Ed was coming to Maine more and more. He had family not far from me— an aunt and a few cousins, including one named Drake who attended my school. Drake was a year older than me and a total burnout. He was sweet but trouble and everyone knew it. He had nicknamed me M&M the year before when we were riding the bus home together.

"Melts in your mouth, not in your hands," he would say and then laugh. It wasn't the worst nickname, I guess, and he certainly didn't mean any harm by it, but I didn't tell Ed for a long time because I was afraid he would knock his block off. One Saturday we were over at Drake's hanging out, and he put a porno in the VCR when we were in the other room. When we went back into the living room and Ed realized what was on he flipped his lid.

"Get that shit off the TV, my girl's here!" he yelled at Drake. Everyone always backed down to Ed. He could be very intimidating when he wanted to, and wasn't afraid of conflict, which made me worship him even more.

Things continued to grow between Ed and me. I could tell he got shit from his family for dating me but he handled it well. He often went into protector mode when he was around me which made me feel like a princess. If we were out to dinner and my knife was dull he would call over the waiter in an instant and ask for a new knife. If I coughed once he would skid the car into the first store that appeared and buy me cough drops. The only other person who ever looked out for me that much was Grandpa Johnny, who made me wear ear plugs and a nose plug every time I went in the pool when I was little, and bundled me up in sixteen layers when it was cold outside. I hated all those things but felt loved by him and this was that same feeling.

I was happy. What made me even happier was when Ed told me he was moving to Maine.

"What?" I threw my arms around his neck. "That's wonderful!" Finally, my other half would be close by and I would see him on a regular basis. His job was over an hour away, but we would make it work. He was going to be taking care of horses, his other passion beside planes. The pay was a lot less than driving, but room and board was included, and he would be closer to me.

Things were great for a while even though I didn't get to see him as much as I had hoped. The horses required a lot of work and he had traded the Delta in for a jeep, which always seemed to break down. But we tried. Ed had even gotten a typewriter and typed letters to me as a way to practice writing since it wasn't his strong suit. I enjoyed getting his letters which he later told me would take him hours to type. They were plastered with correction fluid but I cherished them. It proved he was thinking of me.

Chapter 22

The New Year rolled around and things were good. My grades were up, I wasn't hanging out with Jess anymore which meant I wasn't partying. I'd still swipe a cigarette from Mom here and there but otherwise I wasn't smoking or drinking other than an occasional beer with Ed. Mom had finally given in and bought me a used piano that I played tirelessly. I had even started taking real, formal lessons from the school's music teacher, Mrs. LaSalle, after school on Fridays. I was writing song after song for Ed, though I was too shy to ever tell him or play for him.

Mom and Larry were off my back for the most part, which was a relief. Having Ed in the picture made them treat me a little better, or at least in a more grown-up manner. I wasn't arguing with anyone, and I was doing lots to keep the house picked up since I never knew when Ed would be coming over. Mom had given up any kind of cleaning a few years back and Larry had all but given up trying to keep his house intact after we moved in, so unless I did it nothing got done. I tried talking to them about Doodie's playpen but they ignored me. Doodie was four and didn't play with her baby toys anymore, so Mom put them all in her playpen which was in the corner of the living room. It wouldn't have been a big deal except there were so many toys piled outrageously high they almost touched the ceiling. Besides it being a total eyesore I was worried that Doodie would try to grab a toy and have twenty more fall down on her head. Every time I started going through them Mom yelled at me saying, "Leave it, I'll get to those." I knew she never would but I wasn't going to argue.

Mom still had her meltdowns on occasion but I kept my distance and distracted my sisters when necessary. Larry had backed off leering at me because Ed intimidated him in some way — either that or Ed pissed on some furniture in my house when no one was looking. I wouldn't have put it past him.

"Hey dahlin,'" Ed said as I got into the jeep. He had just picked me up from my piano lesson and we were going to spend the evening together. I hated riding in the jeep because it had a soft top and the passenger side door was broken, so I had to hold it in place the whole time we were moving. It was a two-hand job so I couldn't hold Ed's hand while we were driving around, and the jeep was so loud it was hard to carry on a conversation.

"So, I have some news for you," Ed said. He sounded nervous.

"What is it?" I asked, feeling my chest tighten. I was good at reading him and I could tell something was off.

"Remember how we talked about moving to Florida once you graduate high school?"

"Yes." My heart sank.

"Well, I'm gonna go first and get a place for us, so when you graduate in June you can just head on down."

"Oh, really? When are you planning to do this?" There was no response so I asked again. "When are you planning this, Edward?"

"Next week." His voice was low and he was looking straight ahead. He didn't even finish getting the words out when I started beating him with my left hand, suddenly strong enough to hold the door with only my right arm.

"What the fuck, Ed? Are you outta your mind?" I screamed as my tiny fist pummeled him. "I hate you, you asshole! How can you do this to us?" I was punching him and crying, big heaving sobs until he grabbed my arm to stop me from hitting him.

"Hey, hey... it's okay," he said. "I'm not gonna desert you. I promise. It's just a few months. It'll be fine, babe."

I wasn't buying it for a second. I couldn't believe this was happening to me. My life was going so good, for the first time ever, it seemed. I had let myself get close to Ed and now he was leaving. I wanted to spit on him, light him on fire. How dare he toy with my emotions? Didn't he know what I'd been through? Didn't he know how hard it was for me to love and trust people? I endured the rest of the ride in silence, holding that door. I kept envisioning jumping out of the jeep so I tried to distract myself with other thoughts, like how I would get Ed to change his mind about moving and leaving me. I was too upset to come up with anything brilliant, but I would keep working on it.

"Can you take me home, please?"

"Yes, of course."

I knew I needed to go hole up in my room and have a good cry. I had to get this out of me, so I could move on and feel human-ish again. And I wanted to punish him for ruining my Friday. I wasn't going to spend the evening with him and pretend nothing was wrong. I was never a great pretender, anyway.

I later found out more details about this big move, which was Drake's brilliant idea. He had some friends down in Florida who were making a shitload of money doing construction and had said Drake and Ed could come and crash with them for a while until they found jobs and an apartment. I was even more upset upon hearing this because Drake was a druggie and I didn't want Ed living with him. I yelled and cried and pleaded to no avail. Ed had made up his mind and he was going.

Drake's mom Claire had a small going away party for the boys. Drake was her baby and she was devastated he was leaving. Drake had a girlfriend named Sue who was also bereft, and we three women sat and commiserated about how we didn't want them leaving. Even though Ed loved me (he finally had told me) I could tell he was excited to go. He had dollar signs in his eyes and was happy to get out of Maine, as most people were. I'm sure he was picturing white sand beaches and piña coladas and who could blame him? Well, I could, because it didn't involve me.

Ed promised he would call when he was settled, and he did. I waited for that damn phone to ring for a week — the longest week of my existence. When he finally called I was elated.

"How's Florida? Did you get a job yet? How was the drive down?" I had a million questions. He said he didn't have a job yet but he had a lot of prospects. He was okay with the place they were staying and said he would buy some calling cards so we could stay in touch. After he called I was able to scrape my heart off the ground a little and start to believe that maybe he wasn't abandoning me after all, and that we would be together soon. I imagined jetting off to Florida as soon as graduation was over, regardless of what my parents said. Mom had said I could visit Ed on my spring break which shocked me but put me over the moon. I didn't know if she was on a pill high or really meant it, but I did let myself get more than a little excited about it. Maybe this move wasn't as awful as I thought.

"Hey, Sparrow," Ed said when I came to the phone. I could tell something was off because he almost never called me by my name.

"Ed, I know something is wrong. What is it, hon?" I pestered.

"Hey, so did you ever date a guy named Tom?"

What? *How would he know about Tom?* "Ages ago, babe, why?" *Why is this coming up?*

"Well, Drake and I are staying at his place and he said he used to date you."

I dated Tom in the seventh grade. He was a freshman and we met on the bus. We held hands and once he put his arm around me, but we never even kissed. He graduated two years ahead of me, and came back around my junior year. I went out with him a few times and made out with him once but that was it. I realized he was on drugs and I refused to hang out with him again.

"Hon, it was nothing. I was in seventh grade."

"Well, he says you two hooked up a few times last year. Is that true?"

"Babe, we never shagged, if that's what you're asking."

"He says you did. By the way, how did you date this piece of shit? He's a fucking asshole."

I couldn't believe this was happening to me. I had no idea Drake and Tom were friends.

"Ed, please don't get upset. He's not worth it. Let it go," I begged. Tom *was* a piece of shit. He had turned into a crack head and I couldn't believe he was lying and trying to ruin the best thing that ever happened to me.

"I don't know if I can let this go, Sparrow. It's eating at me." We argued and didn't hang up on good terms. Was Tom Delgado really going to come between me and my dream man? What were the odds?

Ed didn't call for weeks after that. I was upset and felt helpless because he was far away and I didn't have the number there so I couldn't call. I felt myself unraveling again which was unacceptable. I had to graduate and couldn't lapse into some dissociative fugue. I wasn't going back to hanging out with Jess and I wasn't going to smoke a bunch of weed; those decisions had already been made. I was writing in my journal more and also writing more songs on the piano, songs that sounded like 16th century madrigals which I found strange since that was not the type of music I listened to. But that's what came out when I sat down to play. Everything was maudlin and in a minor key.

When Ed finally did call no one was home so he left a short message on the answering machine. It was the last time I heard from him that year. I could say I was devastated but I didn't let myself go there. After a few weeks went by my heart closed right back up like a morning glory, or better yet like a Venus flytrap. I knew better than to let my guard down like that and kicked myself for doing so.

I wasn't mad at Ed for not calling. Instead I convinced myself I was better off without him. For one thing he didn't have a high school diploma. How could I be with a guy long-term who wasn't educated? I decided to let it bother me. I also concluded I didn't want to be the only girl at the prom with a gray-haired date. Ed had mentioned coming back up so he could take me, and I was a little embarrassed at the prospect. It didn't matter that I felt the Earth move under my feet when he walked in a room. That was silly nonsense. I needed a guy who graduated high school and who could spell Sacajawea.

It didn't take long to find one. To be honest I wasn't even looking. A boy at school named Chris had his eye on me for months, begging for a date. We were friends and I liked him but not really in that way, plus I'd been Ed's girl and was devoted to him. When word got around that I was sort of single and in need of a prom date Chris seized his opportunity.

"You're gonna date me," Chris said as he pushed me up against my locker and planted one on me. He was forceful but not in a disrespectful way. I didn't kiss back but it didn't matter. He was making a statement.

After that moment we were somehow officially dating, which was fine with me. I felt like Chris was a much more logical choice, though I couldn't recall when I had suddenly become so logical. But he was my age, wanted to be a lawyer, and came from money. And he was totally into me. He liked to smoke cigarettes and drink, but he did so in moderation. He was from a small town outside Boston so he had some swagger. He was shorter and stockier than Ed but I was okay with not being as physically attracted to him. We were friends and it felt safe.

Mom was surprised that I had a new boyfriend but Chris was also a people magnet so he won her over easily. He had a great sense of humor and he called everyone Joey Bag O'Donuts, so my family started calling him Donut. Larry was out doing his crop dusting and so Mom would let Donut spend weekends at our house. He had a car and we would run errands for Mom; in return she would let us do what we wanted. Typically the errands consisted of running over to New Hampshire to go to Peking, her favorite restaurant, and bringing back enough Chinese food for a small army. Mom had steadily been gaining weight since Doodie was born and didn't seem to care. She still did her hair and makeup on occasion and looked gorgeous, so I don't think she minded much that she still looked pregnant. She wore lots of baggy shirts with stretch pants and just kept eating. I'm sure if she felt fat she just popped one of Dr. Robertson's magic pills, which I always thought would make you lose weight, but not in her case.

Donut brought a ray of sunshine to my house. Ed was kind and lovable but always reserved. Donut was a spaz who loved to poke, tease and keep everyone laughing. He took a special liking to Punky, perhaps because he noticed she was the quiet middle child. He always made it a point to play with her and engage her in conversation.

My house was way more modest than his mini-mansion in Gloucester but he never made me feel less than. Much like being with Alex, I felt loved and accepted. It was like hanging out with your best friend. I wasn't worried if I had something in my teeth or a hair out of place, I could just be a teenager. And he would make the perfect prom date.

Chris loved nicknames, like everyone in my family. He would hold my face with one hand and press my cheeks together and call me Squishy Face. He was obsessed with my round, full cheeks and pinched them often. It was annoying and at the same time endearing. I loved that he was fixated on something about me. It made me feel the opposite of invisible. He felt about me the way I had felt about Ed, and there was something empowering about that. I also loved that he pursued me for a while. There was no way Chris would have dated another girl while trying to date me. I convinced myself that he was the much better choice.

* * *

I surprised myself by being excited to go to the prom. I had found the world's most perfect dress and couldn't wait to wear it. It was a dark mauve taffeta strapless dress with sequins and a train. It even came with Audrey Hepburn elbow-length gloves. When I tried it on it fit like a dream. It even made the rosebuds look larger and fuller. The dress had to be mine.

Mom had actually taken me to the nice mall to go shopping for it, and I was grateful. Unfortunately she had brought the whole family, which was embarrassing but at least she wasn't breast feeding Doodie anymore so that was a relief. Mom liked the dress too but refused to buy it when she saw it cost one hundred eighty dollars. She said our budget was one hundred dollars for the dress and thirty dollars for the shoes. I was crushed. I wasn't working and didn't have any money but I knew I needed this dress in the worst way. It was meant to be on my body. I begged and pleaded but Mom was firm. No meant *no*.

I was devastated to leave the mall without my dream dress. I had never shined in school in any way. I never received an award, never played a sport, never excelled at anything other than French class, but there were no awards for that. I was known for my sense of style and I knew if I got that dress I would have the best dress at prom and my five minutes of fame. I felt like it was owed to me.

The entire ride home I was concocting plans and schemes in my head that would help me buy that dress. I was going to start with Dad. He and Samantha were pretty generous when it came to clothes and I was sure they'd want me to look my best at my prom. As soon as we arrived home I gave them a call. I described the dress to Samantha, and she thought the dress sounded divine. I had gotten my taste in clothes mainly from her over the years and we almost always liked the same things.

"Give me the name of the store and I'll see what I can do," she said.

I was hopeful and prayed to Jesus that night that it would all work out.

Dear Jesus, Please oh please let me be able to wear that dress to my prom. I can't promise I won't drink, or smoke, or shag but I can promise to be the most grateful, happy person at the prom. Please, Lord, don't let me get stuck with some shiny, satin Bo-Peep looking thing that will make me look like a frumpy bridesmaid. I want to have verve and style, like Audrey. S'il vous plaît, Monsieur. Amen.

I felt guilty praying to God for a dress when there were people starving in Africa, but I couldn't help myself. I felt like Jesus and I were friends and that he would understand my need to stand out for an evening. I never asked him for much and I was sure he was glad to hear from me since it had been awhile.

Samantha and Dad came through and bought me the dress. I was overjoyed! It felt like Christmas times a thousand and I couldn't wait until the dress came in the mail. The only problem was Mom felt upstaged and was pissed they had bought it for me.

"Leave it to your Dad to save the day," she said, disgusted with all of us. I was crushed, hoping she'd be happy for me that I'd have my dream dress. Part of me felt a little righteous, though. I had asked her if we could go to the mall by ourselves since I never had any one-on-one time with Mom and she said no. I couldn't recall one time that Mom and I did anything by ourselves. Once when I was about five Mom said she was going to the macramé store and I asked if I could go. "No, stay here. I'll be right back," she told me.

I was bummed and hid in the backseat of the car. I huddled down on the floorboard and didn't make my presence known until she was at least a mile down the road, at which point I popped up and said, "Boo!" Mom screamed bloody murder and we nearly went off the road.

"Sparrow!" she yelled. I thought she'd be happy to see me but she wasn't and it hurt. I'd annoyed her and it showed.

I didn't let Mom kill my prom dress joy and when it arrived in the mail the following week I put it on immediately. It was a little long and the store clerk had said it would probably be quite difficult to hem but I thought she was full of it. I had known of seamstresses working wonders on wedding dresses and I was certain they could make this dress even more perfect for me. If not I was resigned to wearing ten-inch heels if I had to, so I didn't trip over my dream dress. Plus, in a way this was my wedding day, of sorts—my day to stand out, be beautiful and regal. I wasn't thinking of impressing Donut at all because we didn't have that kind of relationship. No matter what I had on he would still go for my cheeks and call me Squishy Face.

Mom reluctantly bought my prom shoes and took me in to get my dress altered. She threatened to back out a gazillion times because she was still angry and not inclined to go out of her way for me. I was walking on eggshells and even resorted to kissing her butt a bit so she wouldn't let me down. It worked.

The night of the prom I decided to go to Chris's cabin to get ready. His mom came up from Gloucester to be there, and we were all staying overnight. Mom had met Eileen and liked her well enough to let me stay. I don't think Mom wanted to see me dressed up for the prom anyway, so it worked out.

I kept my hair down, though I curled it and teased it and shellacked the hell out of it with my trusty Mink. I matched my eye shadow with my dress color which wasn't easy but I had found a shade of mauve that was close. I was alone during my transformation, in the guest room with the door closed. I was sure that everyone's jaw would drop when they saw my getup. The only thing that was missing was my long, elegant cigarette holder, which I had secretly wanted ever since I had gotten the dress.

"Oh, that dress is... *interesting*," Eileen said. She was an older woman and unpleasant at times. She had that old-school East Coast attitude where she would tell you exactly what she thought. I was fairly certain she looked down on me, though I couldn't put my finger on why. She had never been to my house but perhaps Chris told her that I had a gas pump in my front yard, and a dog on a chain with a junkyard dog-looking house. It didn't matter because nothing she could say was going to ruin my confidence or my evening.

"Thank you," I said, as if she had given me the world's biggest compliment.

"I really like it, Mom," Donut said, letting her know she was out of line. "You look beautiful."He approached me and pinched my cheeks, a wide grin spreading across his face. He had gotten me a lovely wrist corsage that matched my dress. I slid it on over my glove and my ensemble was complete.

"Oh my God, that's the most amazing dress!" so-and-so said. "Wow, where did you get that thing?" someone else remarked. I got that all night long. My dress was a hit, which meant I was a hit too, sort of, by proxy. I was content to let the dress get all the glory. After all, I had picked it out. I was the one with good taste. And I wore the thing well. I made that dress come alive, even if no one but me realized it.

Halfway through prom Donut and his friends decided to take our rented van back since they were paying for it by the hour.

"You can't leave the prom," I told him when he promised he would be right back. I knew he was full of it, but I didn't really have a say, so I walked away and they left.

The guys were gone for over two hours. I knew they went to drink beer and get high, and I was irritated. I was left to dance to the slow songs by myself, which meant I sat them out. I danced with a few of my guy friends here and there but that was about it. I was beginning to feel defeated but there was no way I could let myself go there with the most fabulous dress in the world on. So I pulled myself together and made the most of it. I danced every fast song, which included dancing to "Vogue" by Madonna three times. I was the only girl in gloves and I felt as glamorous as Marilyn Monroe. *Screw Donut and screw all boys tonight*, I thought as I made hand boxes around my face and struck some serious poses.

The guys returned in their cars just about the time prom was over. I played the princess card and gave Donut the silent treatment. He was apologetic and smelled like Busch Light. He tried to pinch my cheeks and I slapped his hand away. I wasn't really angry, just proving a point. Later that night when we went to bed he tried to shag and I said no. It was the first time I had ever said no to a boyfriend and it felt good. He didn't deserve to have me that night and I wasn't the least bit interested. Dancing in that heavy dress all night had worn me out, so I turned over, closed my eyes and replayed my glory night in my head. I was out quick, smiling.

Chapter 23

Graduation came in a flash after that. I had gotten my class ring a few months earlier, a dainty gold ring with an amethyst in the middle and a tiny diamond chip on each side. Dad and Samantha had paid for that too, and I was grateful. I felt frumpy when I tried on my cap and gown but there was no way of getting around it.

Mikey was living with Dad and they both flew in for my big day. I had gone to dinner with Dad, Mikey and Donut the night before graduation and Dad had convinced me to move to Iowa in the fall. He wanted me to live with him and Samantha and go to community college for a year. At first I thought it sounded terrible since I had my plan of college on the beach but Dad promised he would buy me a car and Donut reminded me that if I moved to Iowa I would only be eight hours away from his college in Ohio. Mikey had matured quite a bit and I thought perhaps living with him wouldn't be so bad. He was a high schooler now, on the golf and tennis teams. He was even a member of the Young Republicans at his school, which I thought was ironic since Dad was pretty liberal politically. They all worked on me and eventually I said yes. An abrupt change of plans, but the most important thing was that I was leaving Maine. Leaving that house. Leaving the drama and chaos. I had served my time.

Sitting outside at graduation was difficult. I had never been one for pomp and circumstance and this day was no exception. I didn't take the time to reflect back on my achievement because I was antsy for the next stage of my life. For as long as I could remember I had written in my journal, "I can't wait to get out of this hellhole. I can't wait to leave this place." That day had finally arrived.

When the headmaster called my name my heart raced. I wore flat shoes just in case I was so nervous that I stumbled. I wasn't taking any chances with such a large crowd. I took my diploma with one hand and shook the headmaster's hand with the other. I had a flashback of how a few years back he had dragged me to the office by my ear because I had broken the school's dress code and worn jeans with a hole in the knee. Mr. Tuttle was in his eighties but I wondered if he remembered that day too. I was different now. More grown up, more focused. I wondered if he even recognized me.

After it was all over, Dad sprung a surprise on me.

"I have a ticket for you to fly back with your brother and me tomorrow. Go home and pack a bag and come with us, okay?"

"What? So soon?" I hadn't had any time to process my change of plans, and now he was asking me to hop a plane the next day and start my new life.

"Sparrow, just come out for a few weeks. I'll help you get your driver's license, get settled, then you can do whatever you want for the summer. You can come back if you want to." I thought it over for a whole thirty seconds. I'd finally have my driver's license. And a car.

"Okay, Dad. I'll come," I said. I was really doing it.

Donut was staying at my place that night, so I told him on the way home.

"I think it's a good idea. Go get settled, get your license and then come spend the summer with me in Gloucester. I already asked my mom and she said it would be okay."

"Really? She wouldn't mind?"

"No, she's fine with it. We can spend the summer together before we start school. Please say yes." He pinched only one of my cheeks because he was driving.

Chris lived in a beautiful home with a pool, a cabana and a third-story game room that had a bar, pool table and a gorgeous view. He was ten minutes from the beach. He had taken me there one weekend and I was blown away. It was one of the most beautiful houses I had ever stepped foot in. Plus I would get to hang out with my best friend for an entire summer. There was no way I was going to say no.

"Yes," I replied as I grabbed his hand to hold it. For a brief moment I thought back to the plans I had made with Ed, to move in with him in Florida as soon as I had graduated. Those plans seemed ancient now, almost like a dream. I wondered what he was doing, why he never called back. Perhaps he met another Trish who gave good head and looked amazing in a bikini. I felt a familiar sting and quickly put all thoughts of him out of my mind. What I had with Donut was stable and predictable. There was no longing, no heaviness.

I've needed this stability my whole life, I concluded. I knew deep down I still loved Ed, but I had learned to live without people I loved. I learned to live without Mom, without Morris. Some people value love above all things. I had decided to value something different. And who could blame me?

"Mom, I need to talk to you," I said once I got home. I pulled up a stool at the breakfast bar where Mom was sitting and smoking. I knew after I told her my plans she was going to need many more cigarettes and a few of Dr. Robertson's magic pills.

"Mom, I'm going back to Iowa with Dad tomorrow. I've decided I'm going to try college there." Mom was silent for a moment but her eyes widened and her nostrils flared.

"What? You can't leave!"

"Mom, I just graduated. I need to plan my future. Dad's going to help pay for school and buy me a car. Plus, I'll be closer to Donut. It's the right decision." I was calm but firm. I had no desire to fight with Mom or anyone for that matter. I knew I was hurting her. She hated my father, like she hated every man except Frank, Donald, and Dr. Robertson.

For so many years I had to do what she wanted. What Larry wanted. I had to bring in firewood, clean the house, rake the yard, shovel snow, watch the children, fold laundry, and wash stacks of dishes. They had used me. Taken advantage of me. I was done, and it was all hitting her. She wouldn't have her oldest daughter in her pocket to do her work while she sat around smoking and drinking coffee. It must have hit her hard.

"You're not eighteen yet, you can't go." I was a little surprised she had played that card.

"Mom, don't go there. I'm grown up now and I'm meant for more than picking up after you and rotting in this house." I walked away. She knew it was the truth.

I went rummaging in Punky's closet and found the trusty old blue suitcase with the broken handle that I used every time I traveled; the one Mom got with her IGA green stamps all those years ago. I had no idea what to pack so I threw a bunch of clothes in it, along with my set of hot rollers and some toiletries. I didn't know when or if I would be back and I figured whatever I left behind Punky could have.

I brought Punky into my room and told her the news. I could tell she was surprised but if she was sad she wasn't the type to let on. She was twelve, just approaching her teen years and I was sorry that I was going to miss them. I was older and wiser now and I hoped I would be able to give her good advice about junior high and high school.

Doodie was starting kindergarten in the fall and I would miss that too. Doodie and I were still close and I never got tired of watching *The Little Mermaid* with her or playing Barbies. How would I live without these two little humans who not only kept me sane but really were the only true source of joy in my life? My heart began to hurt, so I quickly put all of those feelings in the same box I put Ed in. Sometimes when I let myself swim in feelings like that it felt like I was going to drown, and this was no time for drowning.

"Please take care of Tweak. He's yours now." I told Punky. Tweak was my pet chinchilla whom I adored and had purchased with my very first paycheck from the umbrella store. His cage sat on a little bench next to my bed where he happily ate apples and rolled in chalk dust. I hoped she was happy to have him.

Saying goodbye to Doodie wasn't as tough because she didn't quite understand.

"Sparrow's going to college," I told her. I often referred to myself in the third person when talking with her like Dad still did on occasion. "I'll call you all the time and send you packages in the mail." She seemed excited at that prospect. When I had a daughter someday I wanted her to be just like Doodie. I couldn't believe I was upset when Mom first told us she was pregnant. Doodie was the most precious part of our freak show family. I couldn't imagine life without her.

The next morning I finished packing as I waited for Dad to pick me up. Mom half-hugged me goodbye, but she had a hard time looking me in the eye. I wondered if she had any regrets about the way she had treated me all those years, with the yelling, the coldness, the distance, and her demanding nature. I wondered if she wished she'd gone shopping with me or out to lunch just once by ourselves. I wondered if she regretted paying me in cigarettes to clean the house. None of it mattered. I was embarking on a new journey, and I was starting over.

I said goodbye to all the pets. Seashell, the Australian shepherd mix we inherited from the old neighbor whose house was on cinderblocks. Snoopy, who was still on that chain with the same junkyard dog house. Skye, our pet parakeet who never let me hold her even though I spent years trying. And Tweak, of course, the little guy who never let me feel truly alone even though I spent so many hours holed up in my room with the door barricaded. I was going to miss the freak show family pets. But no one knew better than I that grief is the price of love, so I let my heart feel as much grief as I deemed safe. *A few tears are okay*, I concluded.

Dad honked and I got my belongings together. He sent Mikey to help me with my suitcase which was awkward because Mom was upset I was leaving and sad that she only had a few minutes with her son. Donut had already taken off earlier that morning, and I was glad he wasn't around for my final goodbyes.

I gave everyone one last hug in the kitchen and took a look around. This would be my home no more. I collected as much of myself from that place as I could. In an instant a thousand memories flooded my brain, like watching a movie in fast-forward only one hundred times faster. I breathed in as I let them pass through me and exhaled before I turned around and closed the back door behind me.

Excerpt from Lather. Rinse. Repeat.

"Sparrow? It's me, Ed."

I couldn't speak.

"Sparrow, are you there? Sparrow?"

"Yes, yes I'm here. Wow, it's been what, two years?" Beads of sweat formed on the back of my neck. My heart was racing.

"Yeah, things have been nuts. How are you?"

"I'm fine, Ed. And you?"

"I'm good. I have custody of the kids now."

"That's great. Good for you." I didn't know what else to say, so I waited.

Ed broke the silence. "What's new with you?"

My stomach dropped. I had to sit down.

"Well ... lots."

"Like?"

"I'm getting married." When Ed didn't respond, I added, "In three weeks."

Finally, it registered. "What? Who is this guy?"

"His name's Michael," was all I could muster.

"Well, whoever he is, you can't marry him."

"Oh, really? And why *not?*" As usual, he got my blood boiling.

"Because, Miss Sparrow, you're supposed to marry *me.* That's why."

I was stunned. Of *course* I was supposed to marry Ed. I was supposed to marry Ed and become Mrs. McCue and pop out ten little rug rats. I had wanted that more than anything. But he abandoned me. Twice. I already risked my heart for him and had nothing to show for it but a few old letters and a tarnished silver bracelet. And a very bitter, broken heart that didn't believe in love anymore. I was content to marry a nice man who kissed like a drooling Newfoundland and sometimes finished in his pants before we even got started. And truth be told, he wasn't all that nice, but he wasn't mean and in my world that counted for a lot.

"Edward Joseph McCue, how *dare* you call me three weeks before my wedding day and try to spoil it! Do you think the world waits for you? Because guess what? It doesn't! So unless you want to congratulate me, I suggest you move along." Self-preservation was all I could think about.

"Sparrow, please don't do this. I'm sorry! You're right. I'll do anything, just please don't marry this guy!"

"Edward, the invitations have all been sent. It's a done deal." That's all I could come up with as to why I should marry Newfie Mike and not the love of my life. Was this really happening to me? I had buried him so deep ... again. And now there he was, unraveling me, when I should be thinking of things like how I was going to wear my hair and whether or not I had bought enough Jordan almonds.

"Sparrow, please think about this. You don't have to go through with it. You could call it off. Dahlin', please ..."

There was that melty feeling again. He was the only man who had that effect on me and I hated it. At twenty-two I had grown up a lot. I had two jobs, a mortgage, and I was attending a local college working on my degree. I had quit smoking and drinking and spent what little spare time I had making crafts. I could work wonders with a hot glue gun and a little Spanish moss. I had morphed into the quintessential Midwestern girl.

"Edward, I'm sorry but you had your chance. I'm moving on now and I suggest you do the same." And with that, I slammed the phone down. I was shaking, partly from anger and mostly because that was the first time I had felt anything in so long and it was sensory overload. Instead of having a good cry like I needed to, I reached for Dad's pack of cigarettes and pulled one out. I had been working with Samantha on wedding favors all afternoon at their place when Edward called. I poured a drink, lit a cigarette, and went back to filling little bags with varying shades of pastel-colored Jordan almonds for my wedding day.

For more information, go to http://sparrowspaulding.com/books

16692042R00156